Transformative Selling

Becoming a Resource Manager and a Knowledge Broker

Adam Rapp, Ph.D.

University of Alabama

Sales and Leadership Development Group

Joe Calamusa

University of Alabama

Sales and Leadership Development Group

Daniel G. Bachrach, Ph.D.

University of Alabama

Library of Congress Cataloging-in-Publication Data

Rapp, Adam; Calamusa, Joe; Bachrach, Daniel G.

   Transformative Selling / Adam Rapp, Joe Calamusa, and Daniel G. Bachrach

      p.cm.

   ISBN: 978-0-9897013-3-4

      1. Transformative Selling. I. Title: Becoming a Resource Manager and a Knowledge Broker.
II. Adam Rapp, Joe Calamusa, and Daniel G. Bachrach

Editor: Lyn Maize
Copy Editor: Christy Gold
Book / Cover Design: Anna Botelho

Table of Contents

Foreword

As salespeople, we can attest to the challenges and changes which are occurring at a breakneck pace in business. As educators, we witness the needs of students and businesses in developing and positioning young professionals for a successful career in selling and sales management. As academics, we are keenly aware of the disconnect between empirical research and managerial relevance with real implications that resonate with managers. As corporate trainers, we have seen the litany of models, curricula, and content present in the Learning and Development field. Finally, as strategic business consultants, we have answered the call of many firms in need of direction and guidance developing a sales force competency model, and the creation of a sales force selling capability to enhance their organization's performance.

These roles that we've collectively inhabited have now converged to this point and this moment in time. In the following pages and chapters, we bring our unique perspective to professional selling, presenting real-world strategies and tactics for newly minted salespeople, established sales professionals, and grizzled veterans looking for new ideas or approaches. We welcome you on this journey with us.

Purpose

Of the many companies we've worked with, almost every one has sought our insight into developing a sales capabilities framework "perfect" for their organization. Inevitably, they've asked if we follow the XYZ model or the ABC approach. Our reply is always the same: most popular press books and frameworks look only at one piece of the sales puzzle rather than the whole process. Don't get us wrong; many of the fads, trends, buzzwords, and hot topics that companies ask about contain the nugget of a good idea. But, unfortunately you can't publish a book or build a training program around one good idea. What tends to happen as a result is that great concepts become diluted into 200-page books or three-day training programs, and the "zing" in the original idea is lost.

This book embodies our thoughts and beliefs about the whole sales process, and what makes people successful. As we began putting our ideas together, we knew that we needed to build a comprehensive approach that addressed the entire sales process—from start to finish and every part in between. We also wanted to build a framework that could be used by anyone with a selling role in any organization, was applicable across sales settings, was scalable for an entire sales organization, and would be a worthwhile "read" for someone in a more general customer-contact position. We promised ourselves from the outset of the project that every page of this book would add value to a salesperson's career. We understand the importance of time, and realize that a commitment to read a book must be rewarded with knowledge that can be put to use and have impact on the quality of the lives of past, present, and future salespeople.

Preparation and Grounding

The material that we used to develop the ideas in this book comes from decades of personal experience and expertise. As academics and practitioners, we have had the amazing opportunity to view sales challenges from the perspectives of multiple key stakeholder groups—executives, managers, salespeople, customers, and competitors. As academics we have helped to generate and disseminate the next generation of sales knowledge within the field. Combined, we have authored hundreds of academic articles, conference presentations, book chapters, and books. Over the last 15 years, our research has led us to survey tens of thousands of salespeople and customers and thousands of sales managers and analyzed that data to understand what drives sales performance. We have read and reviewed thousands of academic and popular press articles, and referenced only the very best available information to form the foundation of the sales model we present. We truly believe that there are very specific knowledge, skills, and abilities critical for a salesperson's success and tried to share them here.

As sales professionals ourselves, we have sold to some of the largest global firms in the world as well as the smallest "mom and pop" shops around the corner. We have built training material and exercises and trained executives, managers, and salespeople. Our experiences span many industries and markets—including technology, health care, pharmaceuticals, industrial, consumer packaged goods, and many others—and form the basis for many of the stories and examples we include in the book.

Finally, a point of value, which cannot be understated, is to acknowledge the many others who contributed to this project in both thought and spirit. As we wrote each chapter, we shared it with some of our most trusted friends and advisors in the sales field. We forced ourselves to engage in a chapter-by-chapter, peer-review process similar in many respects to the process that academics go through in the journal article publication process. Although painful at times, we believe that the end product is exponentially better having been vetted by professionals who have both struggled with and perfected the topics we address. We have also shared our ideas over the past several years in our countless sales training engagements, gaining immediate feedback from those hearing the material for the first time. We cannot thank all of you enough who have supported us in this endeavor.

The Evolution of Professional Selling – Raising the Standard

People may ask, "Why another sales book?" If someone does a quick search on Amazon, they would find scores of books covering time management, prospecting, closing, driving the wedge, and so on. What they will not find, however, is a book that takes both a comprehensive view of the sales process *and* that accounts for the radical changes occurring in the selling landscape.

As much as selling has changed, in many ways the fundamental aspects of selling have remained the same. Sellers still need to find prospects, collect research, get prospects' attention, ask questions, deliver solutions, and close sales. What has changed, however, is the rate at which these events occur and the amount of knowledge and insight that salespeople must have today in order to be successful–even in their very first interaction with a prospect.

Taking a minute to reflect on the history of selling, we uncover a timeline that begins long before money was invented. Ancient civilizations engaged in the original form of commerce—

bartering. Although first appearing among Mesopotamian tribes in 6000 BC, bartering has continued as a common practice to this day. In the Middle Ages, Europeans traveled around the world to barter crafts and furs in exchange for silks, perfumes, and spices. Colonial Americans exchanged musket balls, deerskins, and wheat. When money was invented, bartering did not end; it simply became more organized. In 1200 BC, China began using shells as the first form of currency, and later introduced bronze and copper "shells," which were the earliest form of metal coin. Circa 500 BC, the use of coins spread throughout the globe. Later, the Roman empires stamped metal coins with images of their gods and rulers to mark their authenticity, much like the coins we use today.

An interesting dynamic was introduced into the exchange system along with the use of money—skepticism. For years, people who bartered goods or services, such as a basket of spices for a bolt of silk, had a clear understanding of the value of the items in the exchange. When money was introduced into the transaction, so was skepticism. Buyers became wary of the quality of their purchases, leading to evidence of what we now refer to as the price-to-value ratio and objection. Once the challenges of price and quality concerns began to surface in market contexts, business continued to develop and different types of salespeople began to appear. In the 19th century, for instance, the legendary snake oil salesmen grifted from town to town and exploited the unsuspecting public. The "snake oil" they sold was actually only mineral oil and therefore did nothing to remedy the ailments it was touted to treat, such as headaches and chronic pain. Since that time, snake oil has become synonymous with fraud. These early salespeople were followed by the iconic door-to-door salesperson. Although door-to-door sales date back to the "Yankee peddlers" in early Colonial America, they became popular in the early 1900s. The traveling salesperson's stealth weapon was simple—persuasion. "They can make you feel uncomfortable about saying no or good about saying yes," says Walter Friedman, a Harvard historian who wrote *Birth of a Salesman: The Transformation of Selling in America*. "These are the things ads can't do." Door-to-door salespeople only briefly engaged their potential customers, thus had few qualms about living by the principle, "let the buyer beware."

As we all know, one bad salesperson can damage the reputation of a hundred great salespeople. This type of transient selling did a great deal of damage to the reputation associated with the selling profession.

From the late 1970s (when economic reforms were first introduced), outsourcing manufacturing led to low-cost, low-quality providers, particularly importers, emerging in the market, which served to magnify price sensitivity among buyers. Many argued that low-cost providers would only further drive price sensitivity. Business experts argued that consumers would begin to buy solely on price which would ultimately lead to the slow death of the salesperson. However, following history the sales profession evolved by creating new strategies and selling tactics. With the aim of overcoming price-related challenges it became ever more important to build and cultivate relationships with customers, which lead to the emergence of the *customer relationship management* (CRM) approach.

Approaching the 21st century, people again believed that the professional salesperson might become obsolete. With the appearance of the Internet, knowledge was now at our fingertips and the ability to buy was simplified. It was commonly thought that the Internet would lead to a diminished role for individuals spanning the producer and the consumer. However, the Internet and the information architecture it supports ultimately lead to new approaches to selling. Technology allowed sales organizations to segment and target customers. CRM applications gave salespeople the ability to determine customer lifetime value (i.e., a way to view a customer's value over the lifetime of the relationship) and provide services in a way that aligned with customers' value potential. This quickly evolved into the concept that high value accounts require dedicated sales personnel, and the *key account manager* was born.

Today, the shape of the sales landscape is dynamic and continuing to shift. As new challenges emerge, salespeople are prompted to develop new skills and competencies to avoid becoming obsolete. With the availability of vast sources of information, customers have considerably more power than customers of even just a few years ago. This power demands a better understanding of customers' needs *prior* to the sales call. It also imposes more demands on their time and more complicated decision-making processes. It is no longer possible to "sell" to one person. With the evolution of procurement teams and buying centers, salespeople must create portfolios of versatile value propositions. In light of increased time pressures, initial inquiry can no longer be initiated with broad questions like "Tell me about your business," or "What keeps you up at night?" Salespeople are the experts in the sales process, and to be successful they must behave like experts. Sales organizations are introducing increasingly complicated products and solutions, which bring with them higher expectations. These demands require smarter sales, customer goals, and team-selling approaches. Sales professionals must understand how to navigate not only the customer's organization but also the internal sales organization, requiring salespeople to become knowledge managers, knowledge brokers, and information dealers. These requirements are the driving force behind this book.

Our Perspective

At this point, we have revealed ourselves. We believe that there is a critical need for expertise and control of the sales process that depends on thoughtful preparation and planning prior to customer engagement. Preparation and knowledge management are the table stakes to success in the new sales landscape. This is certainly not a secret, but our goal is to provide our readers insights into different ways to manage this process.

We also purport that each step of the sales process has both strategic and tactical elements. We discuss the importance and strategic value of each topic we address, then outline the tactical steps necessary to implement the idea. It is not our intention that this book be merely a presentation of a single idea, or a sequence of checklists to follow. Our approach is intended to help you to take a step back, and to rethink and review your current sales behaviors and reinforce or improve them based on the framework we develop.

We also believe that there is a split between inward-focused preparation and outward-facing behavior. *In its simplest form, sales can be divided into two parts*—everything executed in the course of the face-to-face interaction and everything that occurs outside of this encounter. The face-to-face portion of the sales process represents only the smallest fraction of the critical elements in the sales process, yet this is where most books and training professionals spend their time. Just as a college football team's performance on Saturday is based on the preparation that it has invested during the off season and the week prior to the game, a sale is almost always won or lost based on the amount of work done prior to the interaction, and the knowledge, expertise, and insight brought into the process. In the first four chapters of this book we outline the value of planning and managing information through research and assessment. The following four chapters focus on categorizing accounts and understanding how to allocate resources across those accounts. It is not until these inward-focused skills are mastered, and an expert-level knowledge base has been established that the customer should be engaged.

Organization

We realize the time pressures that sales professionals face, so we wrote this book such that it can be read on the go. It can be read in hardcover, softcover, or on your smartphone, tablet, or computer. You can read one page or the entire book in a sitting. It is structured to suit the time that you have available. Each chapter is broken into smaller individual topics that are free-standing and can be read on their own. Because we know that when a fact is wrapped in a story it is 22 times more memorable than a fact presented in isolation, we start each chapter with a short vignette to provide perspective on the topic.

We also introduce the concept of what we call the "Red Door." The Red Door excerpts are real-world, real-life examples that reflect our own experiences and those of the salespeople and customers we have engaged over the years. Because we wanted the ideas we present to have as much impact as possible, we provide as much grounding as possible in real-life experiences. The Red Door is based on the idea that when you hear a story about a place you've already been, it's the details that bring you back to that place. The excerpts describe the doors that you've already walked through and are intended to take you vividly back. Other features, such as Steps for Success and Call to Action, are designed to isolate key ideas or processes that you can lift and use in your own sales planning.

We have designed the book to focus on key areas, highlighting competencies that we have developed from our personal research, and the decades of sales research. These are reflected in the following areas:

Resource management. In resource management we emphasize the importance of personal development, focused on time management and comprehensive customer profiling. We devote attention to the five factors of internal time management, how to manage external influences, engage in personal goal setting and mapping, and defining the scope, identifying, qualifying, and personifying your customers. Challenges in this competency area include outsider time influence, understanding the path to goal achievement, and visualizing the ideal customer profile.

Knowledge management. In knowledge management we focus on knowledge development and operating in a matrix-selling environment. We outline and discuss strategies for internal analysis, customer analysis, industry analysis, business acumen, buying center roles, selling center roles, buying center behavior, and buying center objectives. Challenges in this competency area include obtaining information and insight, distinguishing real from rumor, finding the needle in the information haystack, navigating the internal environment, and mapping the buying center.

Account management. When considering account management we emphasize the importance of account categorization and purposeful planning. We present a decision matrix and explain the process of placing each account into the specific quadrants of the matrix and how to allocate resources accordingly. The matrix incorporates both supplier strength and account attractiveness while taking into consideration current and forecasted sales. Challenges in this competency area include knowing how to allocate time and resources to various accounts; the willingness to accept that, in accordance with the Pareto principle, 80 percent of your business typically comes from the top 20 percent of your accounts; and that technology can be used to help simplify this process for efficiency and effectiveness.

Summary

We began this project with the goal of creating an inclusive framework that addressed the entire sales process, from beginning to end, touching on all of the processes in between. Whether we change the behavior and life of one salesperson or the perspective of a sales organization, advance the entire discipline, or make the life of a buyer easier, any positive impact will be worthwhile in the hearts of the authors.

We are well aware that many salespeople receive little or no training. Nearly half of the firms in the U.S. have no formal sales training program. One in seven salespeople enters the sales profession with little or no guidance, no mentorship, and very little formal sales education at the university level. We hope this book can be a tool that can provide guidance to these salespeople, or to those veterans facing the loss of ongoing training budgets critical in this dynamic environment.

Finally, we know that too many people criticize sales as a profession, viewing it as just a job. Salespeople are the true drivers of economies and leaders of industry, with nothing happening until something is sold. All businesses and organizations rely on sales and have some form of customer acquisition and selling as their lifeblood. At the end of the day, we are proud of our profession and would like to give back to a discipline that has given so much to us. Now that we have that covered, let's get to work!

Special Feature

As a special feature of *Transforming Selling*, the authors have recorded video introductions to each chapter. You will find a QR code at the start of each chapter. Just use any scanning app on your smart phone to see what the authors have to say.

Chapter 1

Resource Management — Time

"The challenge is not to manage time, but to manage ourselves."

—Stephen Covey

Kim walked to Mike's office with a sinking feeling in the pit of her stomach—she'd gone through this before. As usual, Mike was furiously at work. He was always working. He wasn't lazy. "Ready, Mike?" He looked up like he was coming out of a deep sleep. His eyes didn't immediately focus on Kim. He seemed to be remembering something. "Our client meeting? Fifteen minutes . . . ready?" "Ah . . . Kim . . . I was finishing this project for Pete. . . ." Mike's voice trailed away. He just realized that, again, he was letting Kim down. He was the product expert on this line. It was a major account and the reps were having coffee in the conference room. He didn't have the research done. Why? He didn't play golf. He didn't watch sports. He didn't have any hobbies at all—he was always working. Why did it always seem like he was letting other people down—letting himself down? Where was all of his time going? Good question. . . .

THE PURPOSE OF THIS CHAPTER is to introduce you to a new way of thinking about yourself and the sales process as it relates to your most valuable resource: not money, not intelligence, not social networks, not good looks, and not creativity. In this chapter we emphasize the importance of managing your time effectively. Managing time is critical. Whether you are aware of it or not—and most people are not—everything you do and how well you do it depends on your decisions about time. The choices you make about your use of time every day, either consciously or unconsciously, are critical to your sales success. Without a conscious approach to making decisions about how to manage your time, you are essentially allowing a role of the dice—a random process—to decide your future for you. Our goal is to help you stop gambling—and provide you with a conscious, systematic way to manage your time effectively, to improve your approach to the sales process, and to achieve greater professional success along the way.

Perhaps one of the most important things to know about time management—and most of us do—is that most people are really bad at managing their own time. We procrastinate, we don't organize, we get distracted, and we spend a lot of time on things we shouldn't. For example, on average, people waste two hours a day procrastinating, and 75 percent of us admit to being procrastinators. Office distractions account for two hours of each work day, and people tend to switch their focus away from critical activities after only 11 minutes. What this means is that we tend to use our time poorly, are easily distracted from our goals, and waste a lot of time before getting started. You know what we mean. It's all around us every day.

Our goal in this chapter is to present you with a systematic process to help you become a better manager of your own time. We will explore both internal ("what I am doing") and external ("what is happening around me") factors that play a role in your ability to manage your time effectively. First, we'll go through the various internal factors and external factors systematically. Then, we'll discuss how each of these factors relates to time management and the sales process. Finally, we'll develop key, practical tools to help you change the nature of the contract you personally have with your time, and the way that you approach time management on the job, on a sales call, and in your life.

Internal vs. External Factors

As you make choices about how you spend your time, whether actively thinking about it or not, your choices are influenced directly and indirectly by the situations in which you find yourself.

These include how much time you spend on the telephone, how much attention you devote to any given task, how quickly you start working on a report that's due, or how much time you spend doing research for a sales call—these are important decisions that you make about how you use your time in a particular setting. How you think, what you see (and what you don't see!), how you plan and operate—the decisions you make and how you make them—these are internal factors.

Because none of us operate in a vacuum, everything that you do happens in a setting. In countless ways the setting—the external factors—affects both what you do and how you do it. The people around you, the phone in your pocket, your plans for the weekend, scheduling pressures, your buddy in the office, the doughnut cart—all of these are external factors. In order to understand the time management process, it is important to understand that both internal and external factors play a central role in how this process unfolds. In order to be an effective time manager, you have to account for both the internal and the external factors that influence the time management process.

Internal Factors

Procrastination

In our consulting practice, salespeople ask all the time—"How do I keep from staring at the computer screen all day long, surfing the Internet, and generally wasting time?" This is an important question, and it reflects the fact that most people procrastinate. Sadly, although most people who procrastinate desperately want to stop, they just don't know how to do it. People procrastinate for a number of reasons. For some people, it's because they have a fear of failure—if you don't start on something, then you can't fail. But this becomes a self-fulfilling prophecy. By not starting, you've already failed. Surprisingly, people also procrastinate because they have a fear of success—if they do well on an assignment, there's the fear that more will be expected of them in the future. But this also is a losing perspective from the start because that fear can only lead to failure. People also procrastinate to avoid doing tasks they don't like; but that logic also fails because the longer it takes to get to, and to finish a job that you don't like, the more time has to be spent with it. Often people may not even realize that they're procrastinating because it's become second nature. We waste time unconsciously or fool ourselves into thinking that we're actually getting something done. Unfortunately, one of the consequences of procrastination is that it's much more expensive to get things done at the last minute—pulling in favors, letting other tasks slide, stressing out to squeeze in under a deadline.

The good news is that there are things you can do to avoid procrastination. First, you need to ask yourself, "Why am I putting this off?" If you don't have a reason then just go ahead and do it; and don't confuse an excuse for a reason. Second, set your own unofficial sales deadlines and sales goals. Don't wait for an official calendar timeline—set deadlines for yourself! Third, determine your sales priorities—moving from (1) internal priorities to (2) subordinate issues to (3) customer concerns.

Knowing your concentration threshold is critical to avoiding procrastination. If you give yourself too little time to complete a task—such as finishing a product research report in one day, an unreasonable time frame—you won't start because you know you won't be able to finish. If you give yourself too much time to complete a task, you are unlikely to start because your attention won't last for the duration of the time block you've allotted. You need to leverage your concentration threshold to make the most effective use of your time. This is a three-step process:

1. Know which activity is evoking your procrastination—what are you putting off?

2. Don't give in to the temptation to identify yourself as a procrastinator—this becomes a circular, self-fulfilling prophecy.

3. Determine a realistic time frame necessary to complete the task—accounting for procrastination time.

The next time you schedule a task, allot only the amount of time to that task that you actually need to be engaged in the task. This is your concentration threshold.

To sum up—ask yourself why you're putting something off. If you don't have a good reason, just do it, and don't confuse an excuse for a reason. Set unofficial goals for yourself—don't wait for someone else to set them for you, and prioritize! You also need to understand where your attention goes, and how much attention you have for any given task in order to make effective use of your concentration threshold. This should help you start doing what needs to get done, and avoid the procrastination trap.

> **Red Door: Procrastination**
>
> It's the same on the 15th of every month. You have to generate an aggregate inventory report across all product lines from each warehouse, and calculate a loss statistic for each line cross-referenced—by product—across warehouses. You have to produce and then submit a loss report based on these numbers. You know that no one, ever, reads this report. But you also know that if it isn't on your manager's desk on the morning of the 16th, you'll get a phone call asking for it. You hate this part of your job. You dread it, every month. You know that if you start working on it on the 14th, you'll have it done by the 15th. But every month you put it off until the last minute.
>
> The loss report lingers in the back of your mind, infecting everything else you're doing, or planning. That report starts lurking in your mind around the 10th of the month. You think about it, worry about getting it done, knowing it has to get done. The 13th rolls around and you put it off. You irrationally hope that the report will just go away. You start snapping at your spouse and kids for no reason. You lose your appetite, but drink more than you should. You start to have trouble sleeping, and your world starts to look grey. This report takes up way more space in your mind than it should. It also starts to occupy more of your attention because instead of getting it done, you procrastinate; and the size of the task just grows and grows in your mind until it is all out of proportion with its actual proportions.

That monthly report should be at the top of your to-do list the day before you are planning to get to work on it. Being disciplined about putting it at the top of the list, with a specific start time and time set aside, will help keep you from starting to worry about it too early. There's no reason to worry in advance about something you've got time set aside for. The clenched stomach that starts on the 10th could be avoided altogether if that report had a set time and space all of its own. Every day, leave a clean work space with a to-do list. Leave a sticky note on your keyboard. If you write down what you've got to do and when you're going to do it, you will save yourself the suffering that always comes with procrastinating over that report—or any other jobs you hate—which is always so much worse than the job itself. To avoid procrastination start a task you hate at the beginning of the day—prioritizing it early in the morning will help you get through the task in a streamlined way. You will avoid all of the pain and angst of procrastination and you might even find that the job isn't as bad as you've made it out to be.

Organization

The pitfalls of procrastination are made worse by disorganization—what's left on the desk (or the floor or the chair) that can get lost in the literal shuffle of papers when we leave for the day. Most of us use piles in some form or another as a way to organize our lives. People even keep their most important documents in piles "on that part of the desk" or "that part of the floor." Most people think that their "system" is working, yet they spend a significant part of each day searching, often in vain; 59 percent of sales managers report missing important information because it's somewhere in their office, but they just can't find it. Millions of people have what's called compulsive disorder syndrome, and as a result have trouble throwing anything way—getting literally buried under piles of piles.

Being organized is all about self-realization—knowing yourself and understanding your work preferences. Is your office completely functional—does everything have its own place? Is it somewhat organized, requiring only minimal searching to find lost things? Or is it unorganized with towering piles on your desk and overflowing cabinets? What office environment is your "ideal" environment? Is it a pristine office with a clear desk? Is it tidy and functional with a full but "mostly" organized desk? Do you work best when your office is cluttered and comfortable, with an overflowing desk? Or do you like working on a desk that's too full to navigate easily but where it's sometimes "fun" to discover forgotten items? Being disorganized not only forces you to waste time searching for information, it also may leave potential clients or colleagues with the wrong impression. All that they'll be likely to see when they enter your office is the mess and disorder—not the intricacies of your "system." The Steps for Success box shows several ways to become both physically and mentally organized.

Steps for Success: Becoming Physically and Mentally Organized
1 Create a good file system. This can take a number of different forms. Build a plan to help develop a system that works for you. You can organize by product, by client, by date, by name—but having a system in place is critical.
2 Touch each piece of paper once. If you have to go through items more than once, then they are in the wrong place and need to be filed.
3 Don't leave for the day until your desk is clean. Although it's tempting to say, "I'll clean up tomorrow," piles have their own gravitational force and attract disorder, more piles, and more procrastination. Every day you leave with an unorganized mess on your desk is a day for more clutter to accumulate.
4 Once your work space is clean at the end of the day, leave a sticky note on it with your next morning's task.
5 Stop procrastinating and do it!

The keys to attaining organizational success are:

- Develop a system that you are comfortable with and understand how to use, and then use it consistently every day.

- Take inventory of everything. Make a list of what you absolutely must have in your office, car, or workspace to get your job done. Purge the rest or file it, immediately!

- Develop a simple filing system for yourself.

- Set daily goals for implementing your system, and then stick to these goals—you need to have an organizational plan!

Goal Setting

As a salesperson, it's critical for you to develop a plan to achieve your goals. To be effective, sales goals have to be smart—or better yet, SMART. This stands for:

- *Specific.* You know that you want to increase your sales call each month—but that goal is too vague to be effective. Unless you tag a verifiable, numerical value to the increase (e.g., I want to make 10 more sales calls this month), then you won't know whether you've accomplished your goal. And because you don't know whether you've met your goal, you also don't know what priorities or scheduling you need to change to achieve it.

- *Measurable.* You need to have a way to verify that you've met your goal. You can measure whether you've met a specific increase of 10 calls by keeping a log of your calls each month. Measuring allows you to track your progress, and keeps you focused.

- **A**chievable. If you set a goal that's too aggressive—"I want to increase my sales calls by 50 in the next month"—this can be discouraging. Some coaches call these super-reach goals (e.g., We're going to win State this year!), but if you can't reach the goal then over time it becomes demotivating. So, keep your goals difficult, but attainable.

- **R**ealistic. Realistic means that your goals are consistent with your other priorities. A goal like increasing sales calls is consistent with other professional goals—it won't detract from meeting your other obligations and priorities. In fact, realistic goals help you to reach other professional milestones—they work with your other goals. In contrast, a goal like becoming a professional dancer is probably unrealistic given other life priorities— like becoming a better salesperson.

- **T**ime-based. There needs to be some end-point so you can see where you've come over a given period—"I want to increase sales calls by 10 per month" is a good goal because it gives a time frame for achieving the goal.

In order to accomplish the SMART goals you set for yourself, it is important to engage in goal mapping—which is backing into a sales goal or target by defining what is necessary to accomplish your goals. For example, what steps do you need to take to make 10 more calls each month? Spend less time watching television, stop procrastinating, get up 15 minutes earlier every day, organize work files to take less time searching—all of these steps will give you the time you need to reach your goal. You also need to establish a time frame for the goals you set. Like having a time-base for your goal, you need to understand when you need to do the things necessary to help you to achieve your goal. Watch less television in the evenings, organize files during lunch—this type of analysis will help you take the necessary steps along the way. Having milestones for reaching your goals also is critical. Your goal is 10 more calls each month, and so to start with you are going to get up 15 minutes earlier each day. You hit the snooze once, and only get up 10 minutes earlier—you're on your way, but you haven't gotten there yet. But having a milestone helps you keep track of where you are, relative to where you are trying to get. Finally, you also have to know how the steps you're taking are incorporated into your path toward achieving your goal. What are you going to do with the 15 extra minutes in the morning? If you use them to surf the Internet, that won't get you any farther down the road. If you use them to organize your schedule for the day and send some e-mails that have to be sent anyway, that's more time you'll have toward meeting your goal.

We all set goals for ourselves and get excited when we achieve them. Unfortunately, many of us don't really understand how to actually achieve our goals. To map out the path to your goal, follow these steps:

- Establish your goal and write it down!

- Make sure that it is a SMART goal. Measureable benchmarks are critical.

- Determine your time frame for achieving your goal.

- Set milestones at certain points of time to make sure you are on track.

- If you are not on track, recalibrate your actions, not your goal!

- Share your goals and progress with others who will help hold you accountable.

- Don't celebrate milestones. Use them as "motivation points" and celebrate only the end goal.

Planning

Although people are spending more and more time at work each day, our research shows that most people actually spend 60 percent or less of their available time doing anything productive. This statistic is even more frightening when you consider that 40 percent of American adults get less than seven hours of sleep a night. So, we're not using our work time productively and we're getting less sleep than ever. We all intuitively know Parkinson's famous—but generally unacknowledged—law that work expands so as to fill the time available for its completion. Thus, if we don't plan we end up using all of our time, most of it inefficiently. Time just seems to pass, and we haven't accomplished the things we would have liked to. Although sales planning is a key managerial function, research shows that less than 5 percent of managers' time actually goes toward planning.

Are You a Proactive Planner?

- Do you set aside time for planning?
- Do you set clear steps to achieve sales goals?
- Do you make a prioritized to-do list and get these done as soon as possible?
- Do you use a day planner to schedule sales tasks?
- Do you write down sales activities coming up the next day?

Self-knowledge is critical if you're going to become a better planner. Designate an appropriate time for sales activities. If it's 10 in the morning, it's a problem if you're sending texts to your buddy about an upcoming fishing trip instead of following up on a lead. Prepare a list of daily priorities based on urgency and importance and check items off of the list in that order. *You can improve your ability to plan.*

	Steps for Success: Better Planning
1	Get a desktop calendar—digital or paper—and use it religiously for setting calls and important meetings. Refer to it often and don't let it become "background."
2	Use sticky notes or calendar alerts to keep you focused on urgent and important items from your to-do list. These can cue you to focus on the right things.
3	Use your phone or computer's calendar function to provide yourself backup reminders about important upcoming meetings or calls.
4	Keep your calendar with you! Being mindful to your schedule at work won't help you when you're sitting on your backyard deck or thinking about a long weekend at the lake. You have to keep aware of your upcoming work events at home so you don't double book or lose sight of priorities while you're relaxing.
5	Make sure that you schedule timely appointments—booking too far in advance opens the door to missed opportunities.
6	Get a daily planner—this will help you to develop the discipline to write down where and when you need to be, so you can coordinate your priorities. It is a certainty that your memory will fail you.
7	Don't get caught saying these famous last words: "Oh, I'll write that down later" or "I'll remember"—in our modern lives there are always a million distractions to keep you from doing just that.

Prioritization

What is one thing that you could do—on a regular basis—that would make a tremendous difference in your professional performance? Manage priorities. This means understanding the difference between important and urgent sales activities, and taking steps to focus on *importance* rather than *urgency*.[1] Stephen Covey famously noted that people are addicted to urgency, defining important tasks as urgent and urgent tasks as important. Covey argued that this keeps people from what he called "preventative" thinking, allowing them to get caught up in urgency at the expense of importance. Obviously it is imperative to put first things first and prioritize your daily activities accordingly. However, to do this effectively, you need to understand the difference between important and urgent, and prioritize your tasks accordingly.

The word *urgent* means that something feels pressing, or that it requires your immediate attention. The word *important* means that something is significant to you or is critical to reaching your goals. These key concepts can be combined into four categories of tasks, as seen in Figure 1.1.

Top performers tend to spend between 20 and 25 percent of their time on Category 1 tasks. They spend roughly 15 percent of their time on Category 3 tasks, but less than 1 percent of their time on Category 4 tasks. Not surprisingly, they also tend to spend between 65 and 80 percent of their time on important tasks that aren't urgent (Category 2). Urgency limits your options. Putting "first things first" means that the more time you spend on important tasks, before they become urgent, the stronger your performance will be in the long run.

Figure 1.1. Task Categories

High	Urgency	Low
High *Important and urgent* Category 1 tasks, like crises and deadline-driven projects, require immediate attention.	*Important but not urgent* Category 2 tasks, which include prevention activities, relationship building, and planning, help to eliminate Category 1 and 3 activities.	
Not important but urgent Category 3 tasks, such as interruptions, some calls or meetings, and popular activities, are what are called an "attractive lure" on someone else's agenda—but not **Low** yours.	*Not important and not urgent* Category 4 tasks include time-wasting activities and those items that account for those two hours a day we lose.	

Importance (vertical axis label)

Covey, Stephen. "The 7 habits of highly successful people." *New York: Fireside* (1989).

Red Door: Sales Prioritization

The phone rings. Instinctively, you turn your desk chair away from your project toward the source of the sound. In the split second before you pick up the phone; your eye catches the number on caller I.D. It's the procurement manager at NXT Technologies. You have a moment of hesitation.

continues

NXT Technologies became a customer last year. After chasing them for six months you finally motivated a purchase. You used a deep discount on a product they historically bought from a competitor that maintains a large share of NXT's diverse purchasing needs. The product wasn't really strategically aligned with your organization's plans, and the price was also below cost. But, you convinced management to authorize the sale based on NXT's long-term potential. Once the transaction was complete, you immediately set out to maximize the capability of the account through cross-selling. Over the subsequent six months, you prepared and delivered three proposals to earn an additional share of NXT's total purchasing needs. Although the products you presented were strategically aligned for both companies, competitively superior, and cost neutral, all three proposals were rejected. All the while, NXT continued to submit replenishment orders for the original product, at the original price.

Before the phone rang you were focused on a major prospect meeting set for the following day. You're flying to Boston for a fifth and hopefully final meeting with Adjacency, a global cloud services firm. Adjacency put its entire business up for bid after cutting ties with its previous supplier. Your previous four meetings were tough, but positive. The primary competitor features a product line that seems to match yours at every turn. Adjacency has hinted to you and likely to your competitor that its decision will be based largely on which proposal provides the most creative solutions for scalability. You're sure that this business will be won or lost based on how well you can position your company's solutions.

You have a moment of hesitation as you're reaching for the phone. That moment of hesitation turns into a moment of prioritization. The out-front and unprofitable order on the other end of the phone line will break your rhythm. It will raise your stress level and cut into your valuable preparation time. The alternative is to let the call go to voicemail and to stay connected to the Adjacency project.

Everything you've been taught in sales tells you to answer the phone—you've got a customer on the line. We're taught to service every customer the same way. We're taught to give every situation the same attention. But the NXT order and the Adjacency proposal aren't the same. In this moment you can't give them the same attention. You have to make a decision. Understanding which is more important to your personal goals and your organization's expectations is vital; you pull your hand back. You turn your chair back to its original position. You are invigorated by your discipline. Your focus is even deeper now. Your creativity starts to flow. Tomorrow you'll earn the Adjacency account. The next day you'll call NXT back with a new price and some new conditions for that next order.

Time Awareness

It's critical to be aware of what time means to you—how you feel during different parts of the day. Everyone has periods of what are known as "fast time" and "slow time." You need to know when your creative or thinking time is. For some people it's in the morning and for others it's late afternoon—it all depends on the individual. But, whenever this time is for you, defend it ruthlessly! This is when you are most focused, most clear, and most on your game. If you don't use this time toward furthering your own goals, you are losing your best opportunity during the day to move your goals forward. At the other end of the spectrum, you also need to know when your "dead" time is, or when you're least productive. During this time—which, again, may be at any actual time of the day depending on how you personally work—plan to schedule meetings, make phone calls, do anything that falls into the category of mundane tasks. Only you can figure out your own daily rhythm, to know when your own most and least productive times occur. Knowing this will help you to prioritize, plan, and schedule and execute certain tasks during the day.

External Factors

While the most successful sales managers have learned to expect the unexpected during their daily routine, even the best can succumb to external time pressures or emergencies that crop up during the day. "Priority" items will always appear unexpectedly on the horizon. But, to successfully navigate the external environment, you must recognize these for what they are— external time wasters—and be vigilant when they pop up.

Time Inhibitors

Interruptions, especially in the form of e-mail, are a huge time waster. Workers today spend upward of 40 percent of their time dealing with e-mails, and the yearly cost of time spent on e-mails alone can exceed $20,000 per worker, depending on salary scale. E-mails distract attention from ongoing tasks, and can be especially problematic if these are dealt with during "fast" or productive times. Don't get snared!

Tips for Managing E-mail

Hold off dealing with the bulk of e-mail until your daily dead period. This keeps you from becoming slowed in your progress toward your important sales goals.

- Keep messages brief and concise.
- Don't live on your e-mail—don't let it become a constant backdrop.
- Learn to use your e-mail system. Categorize your e-mails, and divide between work and home e-mail accounts.
- Know why you're sending every e-mail. E-mail is supposed to be a tool to help you do your job.
- Be prudent. Don't overuse e-mail lists or send unnecessary attachments, and be conscientious in subscribing to e-mail groups.

If e-mail starts to get in the way of your goals, it's time to think about how you're using it. Reports are another example of an external time inhibitor. It doesn't matter how many reports you generate if they're ultimately irrelevant toward meeting your sales goals. To be of any use at all, reports have to be tied directly to an established, worthwhile goal. Surprisingly, reporting can lead to a *productivity paradox*. The more successful you are as a sales manager, the more reports you have to read, or generate and deliver to your manager—but the more reports you read or deliver, the less time you'll have available to plan and generate new business, decreasing success! It's essential to identify which reports ultimately are valuable in reaching worthwhile goals, and which are not. Once these have been identified, it's important to follow up with the appropriate people to have the necessary conversations about the reports that are a waste of time.

Meetings

Meetings are an essential part of doing business. Unorganized and especially too many meetings are also potential external time wasters. Although lots of people assume that unless they are regularly having meetings that nothing is getting done, sales meetings are not a "necessary evil." It can be difficult, especially when your supervisor has requested the meeting, but try to say "No" to meetings where you're not required or playing a central role. To avoid wasting time during meetings that *are* necessary, everyone should receive both an agenda and all relevant materials before the meeting (a perfect use for e-mail!). Meetings also should have a scheduled ending time to avoid falling into Parkinson's trap about work expanding to fill time. Finally, important items should always be covered first in sales meetings. This will help to get everyone there on time, and focused on the key agenda items.

	Steps for Success: How Can You Avoid Unintentional Loss of Control Over Your Time?
1	Clarify your role and your expectations (for yourself and your subordinates).
2	Be clear with others.
3	Be explicit that you're not going to take on "monkeys."
4	Use activities as training opportunities for subordinates.
5	Coach subordinates through their problems instead of adopting responsibility for their problems. They'll learn more by doing what they've asked you to do than by having you do it for them.
6	Help your subordinates to become stronger by not letting them avoid what's difficult for them.
7	Offer subordinates activities or projects that they can use to strengthen their skills so that they can be more autonomous in the future.
8	When engaging a person with a task in hand, begin with the end in mind
9	Be mindful of your goals in your interactions with others.
10	Remember that most often people are looking for solutions or guidance rather than for you to accept responsibility for their problems

Delegation

Learning how to delegate also is a key part of becoming an effective time manager. We take on other peoples' tasks for lots of different reasons. We like to be "on top of everything." We think, "It's easier if I just do it myself." Often we take on others' tasks as a result of a time crunch that we've brought on ourselves. This can be explained by the "monkey on the back" analogy.[2] Once we pick up monkeys from subordinates, we send them the message that we want their monkeys. By allowing subordinates to pile their monkeys on us, two things happen. First, we've accepted responsibility for the problem from the subordinate. Second, we've volunteered to provide a progress report for the subordinate.

But, it's important to recognize that delegating sales activities can save you time and help to develop your subordinates' sales skills and abilities. By delegating you can actually help to improve the productivity of your salespeople. You also help to improve results by making use of all of the available intellectual capital and other resources available for the task you've delegated. If you consistently take on others' responsibilities, you are only drawing from a small pool of available talent. Delegating sales activities also transfers initiative and authority to subordinates, which empowers and motivates your employees, and increases their feelings of ownership and performance.

Red Door: Delegation

You're a doer. You've always been the one to get things done in your group or team. You hate to see things slide. It's one of the reasons you've been able to get where you are today, and it keeps you moving and engaged. Part of who you are is picking up the slack for other people. This includes taking on other salespeople's calls when they ask, or subordinates' tasks when they ask for help. But, even though this has worked for you—or you feel like it has—it's risky. You enjoy doing the things you do for others. You enjoy the challenge and it keeps things mixed up and fresh for you. But sometimes we need to stop and think about what it means to use our time for other people, to focus on their problems rather than our own. There are costs associated with helping.

This is a slow process. You like to be "on top of everything," and taking an extra sales call or helping a subordinate to complete a task keeps you at the center of the action. If you help them through what's for them uncharted waters, will your subordinates outperform you? And you decide—like you typically decide—that it's just easier if "I just do it myself." What happens with this approach, though, is that you find yourself running out of time, while those around you are running out of work—because you've taken on their monkeys. You need to get these monkeys off of your back. Once we take on monkeys from subordinates, we send the message that we are willing to take their monkeys—that their work is our work—that our time is their time. We set up a situation where we become the go-to monkey taker, and lose control of our time.

These things take time, which is a restricted, limited resource. Think about your time like you think about your money: you can only spend it once. If you let someone else spend it—if they get accustomed to spending it—that leaves less time for you to devote advancing your own priorities. Delegating saves you time.

The Art of Saying "No"

It's important to recognize that your time is a scarce resource, as well as your most valuable resource. Think about your time in the same way that you think about money. You'd never consider crumpling up a dollar bill and throwing it out the window—you'd have to be crazy to do that! But if you're not an effective time manager, that is exactly what you're doing. One of the best ways to use your time in the most effective way is to learn how to say "No."

Before you decide to take on subordinates' monkeys, ask questions. Think about children's natural tendencies and use their favorite question: Why? Why do you need help with this? Why can't you make your sales call? Why can't you do this yourself? Why are you asking me rather than figuring this out for yourself? Why? Asking these questions can help you be a more effective delegator and can save your time. But watch your tongue! The way that you respond to requests for help can leave the door open for more requests for your time. Saying things like "Maybe," "Let me think about it," "I'll get back to you," "I need to check my calendar," and "We'll see, check back with me" leave you open for renewed requests, both imminently and down the line. Leaving the door open also is much more prevalent with electronic communications. E-mails and texts increase the distance between you and your subordinate, and also offer a feeling of artificial insulation against the time investment you're making by accepting others' monkeys.

Every time you don't say "No," you are giving your time to someone else to use—it's like giving away your money. But it's actually worse because you can't earn back more time. It becomes easier to say "No" once you've clarified your role and others' expectations.

Have clear boundaries, communicate these to your peers, employees and managers, and stick to them. If you do this consistently, then saying "No" is going to get easier. It also is important to realize that a lot of the time when you're asked for your time, or think you're being asked to do something—people are really looking for help finding solutions, or guidance. If you keep your goals in focus, then you may not need to always say "No"—you may actually be able to provide some insight or help without disrupting your schedule and focus.

Technology

When you look at your desk and see your smart phone, your tablet, your laptop, and your Bluetooth headset, it is as clear as day that we are increasingly operating in a technology-driven world. For the most part technology has had a fabulously positive impact on our lives. It is hard to oversell its benefits. But, people attribute a lot of things to technology that it just can't do. People also get caught up in technology, and find ways to use technology for its own sake. This ends up stealing time away from productive goal-focused activities. For example, although technology can help us accelerate momentum toward achieving business goals, it can't create momentum on its own—it's a tool, but it's not a generator of momentum. It's also impossible to make good use of technology until you know which technologies are relevant to your business and which are irrelevant for your business goals. New technology can be extremely seductive. But "having" the technology can become a time drain that gets in the way of other productive purposes if you're not careful. Having the newest gadget and spending all kinds of time learning how to use it may be helpful—or it may not, particularly if it detracts focus away from primary sales activities.

Call to Action: Change the Contract

As we emphasize in this chapter, it's vital for you to understand the role you play in the management of your own time. You must also understand the role the environment plays in how effectively you are able to do this. Time, as your most precious resource, should become your first priority. How you use your time should be central in your thinking. How you manage your time should influence how you think about yourself, what you do, and when you do it. This process starts with the intentional decision to become conscious and focused on making changes—sometimes very small changes—in the way you spend your time.

It is essential to develop your personal and professional priorities. Unless, and until, you know what's most important to you, it is impossible to know how best to invest your time.

Find a tool that you feel comfortable with that you can use consistently—a calendar, a mobile app for your smart phone, sticky notes, or all of these in combination. The key is that you have tools in place so you can develop a systematic approach to your use of time that doesn't require you to rely on your memory. Keeping a time journal, or at least recording the time you spend on different activities, is a good way to begin this process. So, how do you get started? What are the immediate next steps that you can take to become a more effective time manager? In order to become intentional in your approach to time management, it is critical that you understand where your time is going.

Don't postpone your work! Procrastination will always be the antithesis of effective time management, and will steal your time from you as surely as a thief steals your wallet. Identify your time wasters, and resolve to eliminate them from your daily routine—once this becomes a habit, you won't even have to think about it anymore.

Identify the "fast," "slow," and "dead" times you have during the day. Understand your own daily rhythms and select the appropriate tasks for these times. Don't use your most productive time for e-mails and scheduling meetings—use it for priority tasks. Along this same line, make use of committed time—when you're traveling or waiting—to get through mundane tasks.

Have a plan for the day. Make sure that you are moving in a logical way from one task to the next so you can identify gaps and choose how you'll spend your time accordingly. Set goals and work toward achieving these with small steps. You also need to be vigilant regarding where your time is going. Keep accurate records so you'll know whether you're working toward the goals you set for yourself or if you need to modify how you approach your tasks. Note all deadlines in your plans so you have a definite point in the future to move toward.

Make a daily to-do list so you can keep track of your progress. This will help you maintain a record of your progress, and it's also motivating to check things off that list. Prioritize and reprioritize your daily list as you move through it each day. As you accomplish the tasks on your list, different near-term priorities may emerge. Start prioritizing the to-dos on your list into the four categories based on importance and urgency, as discussed above. Work through your top priorities first!

Finally, as we've discussed, you don't operate in a vacuum. Not only is it critical that you take control of all of the internal factors that influence how well you manage time, but you also need to effectively manage your interactions with others—and this involves having some difficult conversations with key players in your life.

Endnotes

1   Covey, Stephen. "The 7 habits of highly successful people." *New York: Fireside* (1989).

2   Oncken, W. J., & Wass, D. (1999). Who's got the monkey. *Harvard Business Review*, 77(6), 179–186.

Chapter 2

Allocating Personal Resources and Sourcing Prospects

"The purpose of business is to create and keep a customer."

—Peter Drucker

Susan headed into work early after an already late night of compiling data to complete the requested reports for the Q2 kickoff meeting. She had met her Q1 numbers and was excited about the accolades coming her way. However, she couldn't keep the thoughts out of her head about how she would meet her Q2 numbers, or the rest of the year's numbers for that matter. Her pipeline was nearly empty and she didn't have any hot leads in sight. She had a few business cards to follow up on but other than cold-calling, she was nearly out of options. Well, she might as well celebrate the morning and lunch since she did meet her target numbers, but the afternoon planning session would be a different story. Rumors were that beyond sales quotas, the firm was implementing something now called a "key performance indicator," which was called customer lifetime value, and they were discussing it after lunch. With that thought, Susan turned up her radio.

SOURCING OF POTENTIAL BUSINESS GROWTH tends to happen in an unsystematic, informal way. Sourcing doesn't obey any well-defined or strategic rules. It often follows an essentially rudderless path, subject to currents and winds rather than proceeding along a well-defined route toward an established goal. Salespeople chase after prospects passing within sight by chance, without ever really considering their overlap with current prospects, their potential lifetime value, their fit with core competencies, or how they'll be effectively integrated into their stable of current clients. We overlook potential growth in current accounts, and blindly chase unknown and unqualified prospects, expending (wasting) valuable time, energy, and effort in the process. Why? Many buyers take a systematic approach to sourcing the products and services that they need. So, why don't sellers source customers following a similar, systematic approach? Good question! Our purpose in this chapter is to deepen your understanding of sourcing, what it means, and how using a scientific approach to sourcing consistently and effectively can significantly diminish your costs and boost your sales success.

Statistics and facts. Understanding sourcing and sourcing effectiveness is a cornerstone to your long-term sales performance. Consider this. Fifty percent of customers are lost every five years due to changes in their needs that remain unmet, new technologies that substitute for current products and services, and competition. Reducing this defection level by as little as 10–15 percent can double your profitability. What's more, the effort and resource expense that is needed to capture *new* customers is almost six times higher than that necessary to retain *existing* customers. In addition, loyal customers—or partners—spend five times more than indifferent customers on annual maintenance, upgrades to current offerings, and additional products and services. In light of these striking numbers, a salesperson's goal for any prospect, customer, or partner is to maximize lifetime value.

The objective for this chapter is to shed some light onto the sourcing process, offering a systematic approach to help you manage the sourcing process more effectively and consistently. First, we'll go through the sources from which customers emerge and discuss the differences between prospects, accounts, and partners. We'll explore the ubiquitous sales funnel and introduce the notion of the inverted funnel, and spend some time discussing common misconceptions about the best form and configuration of the funnel, customer relationship management, and customer lifetime value. We'll introduce you to a systematic process for sourcing, defining scope, segmentation, and source identification. Finally, we'll go through the concepts of source target qualifying and personifying, and discuss the buying center.

Sourcing Prospects

Sourcing refers to the process of identifying valuable and qualified potential customers. Potential customers emerge from three possible sources—prospects, accounts, and partners. Each of these is associated with different costs and potential value.

Prospects are potential, untapped, future value. A prospect is any qualified potential customer that has buying authority or is a decision-maker in a position to give you a "thumbs-up" on a purchasing decision(s). Prospects are different than leads. Leads include business cards, contact lists, and some referrals. Leads don't know who you are. They haven't given you permission to contact them or to provide them with information about your product or service. A prospect, however, has given some type of permission for you get into contact, and is interested enough that he or she would not be surprised to receive information from you. Prospects include web visitors, incoming e-mails, and solicitations for information or an appointment, and have moved past the point in the sales process of being just a lead. Understanding the difference between a prospect and a lead is an important if you want to expend your scarce time and effort in the most effective way. A prospect represents *potential*. They are not currently purchasing from you and contribute a zero share to your current buying and selling volume. It rests on you as a salesperson to transform their budding interest into a purchase decision—or an account—which takes time, effort, energy, and expense.

Accounts are different. Accounts are currently purchasing from you, and have moved past the point of being prospects as they have actually made an investment in you, but their investment made in you is neither predictable nor reliable. They do not consume your product or service to their fullest available potential. Accounts also do not represent a dominant share of your buying or selling volume.

Partners are more than accounts. As they provide more information about themselves, they become increasingly loyal and continue to drive your sales and profits upward. Because of the potential they represent, every interaction with a partner should be viewed as an opportunity to add value. Interactions with partners should be approached with the express intent of deepening the relationship. You should approach partners, not with the goal of merely "selling" to them but with an emphasis on "serving" them and their needs as you would in a consultant role. It is critical here to recognize that developing long-term relationships with partners is not just another strategy for competing, but is quickly becoming the *only* viable strategy. You inform partners, you educate them, you guide them, and you help them grow in their understanding of the ways in which you can help them to generate more business.

Sales Funnel

Many salespeople have been "brought up" with the idea of the sales funnel, which is wider at the top than at the bottom. Every salesperson understands this idea. It is a taken-for-granted aspect of the sales process and a cornerstone of learning to sell. The sales funnel is based on the notion of the "close rate" or "ratio number," and tells us that we should develop as many "hot leads" as possible to build a wide top-end of the funnel. A fraction of these leads then become "opportunities" (i.e., as the funnel narrows), a smaller percentage of these become proposals or quotes (as the funnel continues to narrow), and finally an even smaller fraction of these become "new customers" (with the narrowest part of the funnel at its base). A common saying is that for every 100 hot leads (wide funnel mouth) that one sale will emerge (narrow base). A lot of attention has been paid to the shape of the sales funnel with a focus on the velocity of each stage—or the speed between stages, which is reflected by the steepness of the funnel.

The wider the funnel—or the larger the first phase—the less efficient the process of moving leads to customers—the more time, effort, energy, effort and expense is involved in generating each new customer. The steeper the slope moving from the first phase in the process to the final phase, the higher the velocity at each stage, the more efficient the transformation process, the lower the per-customer cost for the salesperson. However, even keeping the outdated idea of a "funnel" reflects a crucial misconception about the most effective way to source customers in the first place. If salespeople adopt a systematic approach to sourcing, the walls of the funnel can become vertical. Although this notion is perhaps somewhat incendiary, when the funnel becomes a cylinder, essentially *every* "hot lead" becomes a new customer. The effect of adopting this approach is to fundamentally increase the effectiveness (or percent of target met) at each stage, diminishing or eliminating friction in the process of transformation.

Inverted Funnel Concept

Today's sales success increasingly requires that we shift our framing away from volume toward a focus on customer lifetime value (CLV). In other words, not only increasing the number of customers, but also increasing the value of those that we currently have. Recognizing this evolution, we introduce the idea of the *inverted funnel*. We believe that effectively developing and nurturing long-term relationships with customers is not merely just another strategy, it is fast becoming the only viable strategy. In light of this contention, and the focus on CLV as the core evaluative criterion, we turn the traditional idea of the funnel on its head. In the inverted funnel, a smaller number of customers enter the top of the inverted funnel as a direct result of the sourcing process we propose. The wide bottom of the inverted funnel essentially represents increased lifetime value generated from these smaller numbers of customers. This geometric shape reflects our focus on a systematic, scientific approach to sourcing that focuses on per-customer derived value as a key outcome.

Red Door: Better Leads versus More Leads

You're working, and all of a sudden, you get a call. Your boss wants to see you in his office. He tells you, with concern, that he just finished reviewing your sales pipeline on the dashboard of the CRM technology system. The pipeline is thin. He tells you that the number of leads into the system is low. The leads don't meet the benchmark numbers. Before you respond, you take a mental step back. You carefully consider your next few words—they could be really important. . . .

Last year your firm implemented a new technology system. It was supposed to make your life easier. Top management touted the system. They claimed that the new technology would make your sales calls "more effective" and "more efficient." There were months of implementation challenges, Following training session after training session, in the end you were totally bogged down with it—logging more and more information into the system. What was touted as a tool to improve efficiency and effectiveness ultimately become a tool for "big brother" to track your sales calls and customer contacts. At times, you feel like all you do is put more and more information into the system in order to meet reporting requirements set by your manager.

When you first came to work at the company, one of the key performance indicators was the number of leads in your sales pipeline or "funnel" as your boss called it. There was always a lot of talk about firm conversion rates. The talk focused on the number of leads you needed to get one appointment, and the number of appointments you needed to write a quote, and the number of quotes you needed to make a sale. For some (arbitrary?) reason, it was determined that it was always a 10:1 ratio to convert prospects to the next step in the process. They told you that in order to hit your monthly target sales you had to have a huge number of leads in the system at any given time. With the new technology in place, it was easier to track your leads and take you to task on it.

As you prepare to respond to your boss about your lead "shortage," you take a moment. That moment of hesitation turns into a moment of clarity for you. Although you don't always have the "right" number of leads in the system, you've never missed your target sales number. More times than not, you're in the top 10 percent of the firm. You realize that you could give the same old explanations or excuses as to why you don't have the required number of leads in the system. But, you decide to take a different tack this time.

Everything you've ever been taught in sales essentially proclaims that there is some kind of predetermined conversion rate, and that the more that goes into your sales funnel, the more that comes out. While that truism might be the case in some industries, it may not be true for you. You know that you have more accounts, and partners, that will buy again—and buy more—than a brand new lead. You realize that the sales cycle with these partners is much shorter, and that you can hit the majority of your sales target by leveraging your current relationships. While you know that some business will come from new leads, and that future revenues rely on generating new accounts, you don't subscribe to or follow a "numbers game" strategy. Better planning and preparation has enabled you to be more effective and efficient, and to reduce the taken-for-granted conversion rate everyone talks about. This is the conversation you have with your boss.

Customer Relationship Management and Customer Lifetime Value

Customer relationship management (or CRM) is a process for managing customer information. This includes managing all of your customers' "touch points," which is where customers encounter your brand, your product, or personnel associated with your brand or product. Taking control over touch points lets you create and maintain a consistent experience for customers, therefore aligning your tactical approach for each customer. CRM is a strategy that hinges on a salesperson's up-front preparation. The more information you are able to generate about the ways customers interact with various aspects of your product or service, the more consistently you'll be able to tailor your approach to match their specific current and future needs and goals. Any information that helps salespeople to attract and to retain customers is valuable for CRM. Four principles underlie successful value creation programs, and they all relate to the role information plays in this process. The better salespeople know their customers, their competitors, and the market, the greater the likelihood that they will be successful. It is important to recognize that today's customers are more sophisticated than in years past, and they are less susceptible to the influence of the market. A successful approach requires an authentic awareness of customers' specific needs and goals. Thus, a customized sales program can only be effective if it is based on relevant information. Finally, it is critical to acknowledge that value has a much more powerful influence on customers' buying decisions than image. For today's customers, it isn't enough for solutions to have a fancy label, or be the approach du jour—the solution actually has to be functional and relevant given recognized or implicit need.

When you consider how increasingly difficult and costly it is to develop new customers, it becomes clear that a salesperson's goals for any prospect, customer, or partner should be:

- To maximize that customer's lifetime value.

- To make sourcing decisions based on that customer's predetermined CLV calculation.

CLV is the net profit earned from a customer during their time as a customer with you. A customer's estimated lifetime value should be the basis for how you approach customers. It should influence how you source, and should be a primary driver of the decisions you make about how you use your time and expend your resources toward this end. It is useful to compare the idea of CLV to return on investment (or ROI). Return on investment reflects the results of a salesperson's immediate sales effort. In contrast, CLV makes use of relationship capital that the salesperson has developed over time to capture the long-term value of each customer. Mediocre salespeople focus on generating revenue; outstanding salespeople focus on generating profits and make sourcing decisions based on anticipated value.

So, how is CLV developed? It is developed by acquiring a customer through systematic sourcing and attention. What is involved in systematic sourcing and attention? A lot of things:

- Making a connection and building relationships.

- Increasing revenues through cross-selling and up-selling.

- Retaining customers by providing customized service and innovation based on customer-specific information.

- Increasing profits by leveraging economies of scale and effective resource allocation.

- Reducing costs associated with acquisition and recurring business.

CLV rests on the understanding that although we may sell to a customer at one point in time, we consult and manage relationships with customers (or partners) forever. The potential upside of CLV ends when customers defect. Some customers are attracted to competitors, who are more attentive to their current needs and aspirations. Some customers are lost when we fail to continually refresh the value associated with products and services. Some customers move, and some are pushed away unintentionally or intentionally—all of which diminish CLV. CLV can be improved by:

- Understanding—and then acquiring customers with high potential lifetime value.

- Being careful and selective in approaching prospects.

- Introducing new solutions to current accounts.

- Ensuring that the services that you provide continue to meet both their current and expected future needs.

- Aggressively pursuing growth, making growth a natural extension of the current relationship, and managing resources (such as information and time) effectively.

Building a Systematic Process for Sourcing

In order to realize the potential of a sales funnel with an essentially vertical slope and maximum velocity moving from lead to customer—the sales cylinder—it is essential to build a systematic, efficient sourcing process that reduces front-end resource waste. Sourcing, like every part of the sales process, is controllable. Sourcing also depends on your attention to decisions at each of several stages of the sourcing process—selecting the environment in which you'll operate, and shaping that environment to most closely match your capacities, rather than succumbing to the environment in which you happen to find yourself. You can think about the sourcing process as a pyramid, with a wide base and a narrow peak.

For most salespeople, the foundation of their customer sourcing involves an essentially random identification of prospects. The majority of most salespeople's sourcing comes from finding prospects, which is the most inefficient possible means to source. Although prospects have shown an interest in your product or service, converting a prospect to an account is expensive, time consuming, and very uncertain. Prospects have yet to become actualized potential. They haven't actually contributed anything to your buying and selling volume—and yet this is where most salespeople spend most of their time and effort! Moving up from the base of the pyramid, most salespeople spend the next largest chunk of their sourcing resources on current customer accounts, and the smallest percentage of their time on partners. This represents wasted effort and time. In order to generate maximum CLV, salespeople should be spending the least amount of time finding customers—building the base of the pyramid should be completed as quickly as possible. The most productive use of a salesperson's resources comes first from catching customers (i.e., converting prospects into accounts), and then keeping them for the long term. Transforming current accounts into partners, by increasing value and finding ways to meet either expressly defined or implicit current or future needs maximizes CLV. Chasing hot leads does not.

Defining Scope

Making the transition from spending time chasing leads to selling more to current customers and developing long-term, value-producing relationships with partners—sourcing effectively—starts with defining the customers that best fit the characteristics of the services or products that you can currently supply or have the ability to supply in the future. Doing this gives you the potential to influence the shape of your sales funnel, and to substantially improve the conversion rate you are able to achieve as a result. The goal is to transform your sales funnel into a cylinder, maximizing transformation velocity in the movement from prospect to partner. Defining scope starts with the creation of an ideal customer target profile through what we call "CAN" modeling. CAN modeling encompasses three underlying attributes—the Characteristics of the target, the Activities of the target, and the Needs of the target. In some ways, the CAN model is similar to the formula used by social dating sites that help people today. The critical variable in this process is the creation of a match between you and "someone." In the search for a connection, you're first going to pick the characteristics of a person that are likely to be the strongest drivers of long-term happiness (i.e., lifetime value). You might be interested in someone who's attractive and intelligent, with good values, and who has a sense of humor. These characteristics are what you're looking for. You won't read profiles of someone who's unattractive, or who doesn't appear to have good values—that would be a waste of your time. The same fundamental theory applies when you create an ideal customer target profile.

In order to establish your target profile you need to know what characteristics are critical for you to see in a customer.

- What are their sources of revenue?
- What is the structure of their organization?
- Who are the decision-makers? How many employees do they have?
- Does the organization have sufficient importance to make it attractive?
- Who are their customers?
- Are they likely to be available for multiple products or services?
- What markets are they in?
- Do these characteristics coincide with your points of tactical strength?

All of these characteristics have to be in alignment with your ideal customer profile before it makes sense to invest resources in pursuit. However, understanding the characteristics of your "optimal" customer is only a starting point.

You also need to know in what kinds of activities your ideal customer is involved—just as you would a potential partner. For example, you may have found an attractive, intelligent, funny person with good values who isn't at all interested in your interests. This person may look great on paper, but you like to spend your time climbing rocks and riding motorcycles, and this person likes to spend time reading and lying on the beach. Based on characteristics alone, this seemed like a match. But, based on what this individual likes to do—his or her activities—this is a nonstarter.

Just as you wouldn't waste your time with a beach reader, it's also critical not to waste your time pursuing a prospect whose activities don't coincide with your target profile.

- What are the prospect's business objectives?
- What are their core competencies, weaknesses, strategies, and plans?

It's critical to understand what these activities are before expending time, energy, effort, and other resources pursuing a beach reader who's unlikely to enjoy getting on the back of your bike and/or going rock climbing.

Finally, to know whether a prospect fits your target profile, it's also essential to know what *their* needs are before making any kind of investment in pursuit. From our dating example, if you've found an attractive, funny, smart, motorcycle-riding rock climber, before you buy a ring, you'd better know whether he or she is interested in dating. If all he or she is looking for is making "new friends" or becoming "climbing buddies," then you'd be wasting your time getting too involved. If he or she is interested in "dating" or a "romantic relationship," then your efforts are more likely to be justified. Likewise, it's critical to understand the needs of any prospect before you decide to actually pursue them.

- What are their internal and external opportunities and threats?

- Does what you're positioned to offer them coincide with their needs? If not, then spending time chasing after them would be wasted.

If so, then this would be time well spent. Defining scope in this way prior to expending resources in pursuit of "hot leads" functionally reduces the diameter of the sales funnel, increasing conversation rate and transition velocity. Figure 2.1 is a simple example of a tool that you can use for this CAN modeling exercise.

Figure 2.1. CAN Modeling Exercise

List out Ideal Profile **Characteristics**	Prioritize 1–4
1.	
2.	
3.	
4.	
List out Ideal Profile **Activities**	Prioritize 1–4
1.	
2.	
3.	
4.	
List out Ideal Profile **Needs**	Prioritize 1–4
1.	
2.	
3.	
4.	

Segmentation

Once you've created a target customer profile that is consistent with maximizing CLV, it's important to segment your market in order to organize your target search in a coherent way. Within markets, it's always possible to "cluster" customers into similar groups. Segmentation involves dividing target markets along lines at key points of distinction. Traditionally these segments are based on, or defined by, characteristics such as income or demography or web usage frequency. Segmentation distinctions like these are very broad, and are not reflective of the CLV frame definable through CAN modeling. Using a broad segmentation approach like web usage to differentiate between potential customers is akin to a search on a dating site based on someone's age and education. If you read all of the profiles of prospective mates who are attractive, under 40, and have a college degree, you haven't narrowed your funnel sufficiently to be effective. If you search for attractive, under 40, college educated, *and* living in your town, you'll have narrowed your funnel. "Living in your town" versus "living in Wisconsin" is akin to a distinction between internal and external segments. Once an ideal target customer profile has been established, it's possible to segment more specifically using your CAN profile as a point of departure.

Internal versus external segmentation offers a way to significantly narrow the diameter of the sales funnel toward the ideal cylinder configuration (i.e., living in your town). Within your *current accounts* are customers who meet the criteria established employing CAN as a means of authentication—and there are those that don't meet this standard. You've already invested significant time, energy, effort, and other resources to pursue and capture these customers. The front-end investment necessary to transform these prospects to accounts has already been made. Because there's already a substantial investment there, the percentages are much higher associated with the further transformation and development of these CAN-authenticated, internal customers into partners, than for either external CAN-authenticated prospects, or current accounts that don't meet the CAN criteria.

Puppies love to chase balls around the yard, and they'll chase the ball with you for hours. But if a squirrel runs by, they'll be just as happy running after that squirrel, even though they have no chance at all of catching it. The puppy principle makes clear that dogs will chase everything. Salespeople, however, must prioritize based on the possibility of converting. For most salespeople, as soon as there's a hot lead, their attention shifts like a puppy's attention from a ball to a squirrel. Adopting a disciplined adherence to an exclusive focus on CAN-defined internal targets helps salespeople to avoid falling prey to the resource losses associated with chasing hot leads. How do you make this happen?

Information is the key to making sophisticated decisions about where to expend resources. It is critical to work with any and all available knowledge about accounts, partners, and prospects so time and energy are focused toward targets most likely to convert. Sales force automation (SFA) is one of the tools available to increase accessible information about customers and potential customers. SFA both broadens your reach to more CAN-defined internal customers, and also increases the richness of information about each of these targets. Because this increased richness provides salespeople with access to more information about customers, it can help you make decisions about your resources that align with your CAN criteria. The results of this include increasing conversion rates, and decreasing per-customer resource expenditure.

Finally, although CAN modeling can help you to generate an "ideal" profile, it's important to remember that there's probably no such thing as the perfect prospect. You may be searching for an attractive, tall, fit, funny, well-educated, rock-climbing, motorcycle enthusiast living in

Madison, Wisconsin, who has traditional values, likes to drink beer, and is also looking for a romantic partner. But, you also have to recognize that this particular person—one who meets all of your specifications—may not exist. Although you might have a perfect mate in mind, in order to narrow the field down to the best choice in light of what is available, you also have to prioritize the CAN factors you've identified.

What are the most important attributes for a target?

First, the target's needs have to include products or services that you are able to provide or that you can source effectively in a cost-efficient way—your prospective mate has to be looking for a partner—or else there's no reason to engage in pursuit. Understanding a target's needs only happens when you engage in a disciplined front-end information search, which can save a great deal of time and effort by not pursuing targets who are only looking to be friends. Prioritization based on needs represents a first cut that can reduce the diameter of the top-end of the sales funnel. Recognizing your *own* requirements is also an essential part of establishing CAN priorities.

What level of fit is necessary between the products and services you offer and the target's activities?

The CLV that is ultimately necessary to make it worthwhile for you to pursue a target also highlights the need to focus on a target's characteristics as well. The potential business a target represents has to be taken into consideration—but ultimately may be less relevant than whether a target's activities align with your core capabilities, or whether the target will benefit from these capabilities. When segmenting, it's critical to understand not only your own requirements and needs (what value makes a prospect worthwhile), but also to weigh this value assessment against your capacities and a target's needs.

Identify

Once you've established the configuration of your ideal target prospect, and prioritized to create a realistic set of "must-haves" versus "would-likes," these form the basis of sourcing in a way that increases the velocity of transition from prospect to partner (i.e., transforming the sloping sales funnel into a vertical cylinder), but they are not enough. You also need to identify targets consistent with your CAN match list. *Traditional* target sourcing is driven by attention feasibility. Attention refers to the process that someone (a potential target) uses to choose from among various alternatives (salespeople) that strike their senses at any given moment. Attracting the attention of potential sources means making a connection and building a relationship. Sourcing that follows the traditional approach involves attracting and retaining the attention of essentially randomly identified potential targets (e.g., squirrels running across the yard) through referrals, networking, and database searches. Traditional, ad hoc sourcing approaches of this kind don't offer the critical value derived from purposeful target identification using C^2 methodology. They don't narrow the funnel. They don't increase transition velocity. They don't increase "close rate."

The *C-Squared* or C^2 method of target identification is strategic in that it systematically reduces the time, energy, effort, and other resources that you expend in the pursuit of prospects, and ultimately as a consequence in the generation of accounts and partners. C^2 stands for:

Current Customers

Customers' Competitors

Competitors' Customers

Implementing C^2 requires a disciplined approach to target identification. First, your current customers represent an investment that you've already made; the time and effort that you spent to capture them and then to develop and maintain a productive, ongoing relationship. Applying a rational approach to resource allocation decisions reminds us that although a sunk cost is one that has already been incurred and cannot be recovered, this cost also represents a relationship than can be leveraged and can provide you with access to information and other potential contacts. Further, if you think about the goal of transforming accounts into partners, current customers also may actually represent a fixed sunk cost, or a continuing investment that can be further leveraged to deepen and expand current relationships.

In adopting the C^2 method:

- Current customers should always be where you look first for sourcing. Your up-front investment has positioned you to approach this group from a position of strength based upon customer information as well as relational (or attention-based) feasibility.

- Focus on the best accounts with the highest current utilization first. These accounts should be at the top of your priority list. Star customers have both high current value and a willingness to engage that increases their probability of both current value retention and future value growth.

- It is critical to approach current customers, whom you know best and who also are most familiar with you and your products and services, with an opportunistic focus on their strategic development and an eye toward increasing their value—that is, the tactical transition of accounts into partners.

A simple tool that you can use to complete the C^2 approach is shown in Figure 2.2. If you combine the exercise with the earlier CAN exercise, you can begin to generate a high potential list of prequalified sales leads.

As we can see in Figure 2.3, close behind current customers in the list of potential targets with the highest potential utility are your current customers' competitors. These targets allow you to leverage the knowledge and understanding you've generated through the servicing of customers with similar characteristics and engaged in similar activities. In order to target these customers' competitors, consider the following steps:

- Devote effort to understanding your customers' competitors' needs. Although they compete with your customer, you don't know whether they have similar levels or types of needs as your customer, so you must seek out that information.

- Focus on those customer competitors to whom your core competencies and infrastructure are easily transferrable. It's important to remember that while there may be overlap between current customers and your customers' competitors, it is critical to not lose sight of CAN modeling in this process.

- Keep size in mind. If these competitors don't fit—if there is a poor match between their processes and your capacities—a disciplined sourcing approach requires that you pass on these targets.

- Leverage the similarities across these accounts to create efficiencies in gaining their attention and securing favorable appointments.

Figure 2.2. The C² Approach

Potential Customer List

	Characteristics					Activities					Needs				
	1	2	3	4	5	1	2	3	4	5	1	2	3	4	5
Current Customers															
1.															
2.															
3.															
4.															
Customers' Competitors															
1.															
2.															
3.															
4.															
Competitors' Customers															
1.															
2.															
3.															
4.															

Figure 2.3. Identifying Targets with the C² Method

1. Current Customers

- *always the first look*
- *star customers with highest current utilization*
- *opportunistic development strategic approach*

2. Customers' Competitors

- *maintain integrity of CAN modeling*
- *provides efficient attention process*

3. Competitors' Customers

- *maintain integrity of CAN modeling*
- *provides efficient qualification process*

Personify
Qualify
Identify
Segment Market
Define Scope

Finally, third on this list of potential targets are your competitors' customers. Again, it is vital to use the CAN modeling approach you've established. But, if these criteria offer a match following CAN modeling, this target class represents the opportunity to generate value for you and for your firm. To do this:

- Identify your current competitors.
- Ensure a clear overlap in need—i.e., services and products currently purchased from your competitors that you are positioned to supply—so your current infrastructure can be leveraged.
- Leverage the similarities across these accounts to create efficiencies in qualifying these targets.

Red Door: The Trade Show

You've struck gold! You've been standing in front of this elaborate trade show booth for eight straight hours, but it has finally paid off. In your hand is a stack of business cards that must be three inches thick. Every card represents sales growth. You scan around the show floor, wondering if the dozens of other vendors had as many visitors as you had today. "No way," you think, "look at my stack of cards." The only thing standing between you and all-but-certain new sales is whether you can figure out how to disassemble this booth.

The next morning your pace as you go through the normal office routine is quicker. There's nothing in sales quite as motivating as a list of prospects just waiting to be called. By 9 a.m. you're ready to attack the opportunities that visited your trade show booth yesterday. You grab a card from the top of the stack, then pick up the phone and dial the number . . . voicemail. The next card . . . assistant answers . . . to voicemail. Two more cards, two more voicemails. Then finally you get an answer: from Jason Hodges at Global Express Technologies. You remember Jason. He stood at your booth for 20 minutes nursing a cup of coffee, sharing stories about his family. He was excited about his team's chances in the playoffs, and had a lot of ideas about the upcoming local elections. You start the conversation by referencing his family, and the rapport building continues. After a few minutes you adeptly transition the conversation to the new product you were featuring at yesterday's show. Just as you are moving into how your product can significantly cut costs, you notice that Jason hasn't said anything for a couple of minutes. This seems to be unlike Jason. You check in by asking him if everything you've said so far makes sense. His response totally surprises and deflates you: "Man, Global is on a completely different platform than what you're offering. We honestly couldn't implement it even if we bought it. They make me go to those trade shows as part of our ongoing learning initiative that came down from Human Resources. Heck, I don't complain because it's a paid day out of the office. But, if you've still got access to those playoff tickets. . . ."

You're beginning to wonder if it's "fool's gold" you struck at yesterday's show. Now that stack of cards looms heavily on your desk, like a common work task list. "I've got to call all these people?!?!," you think to yourself. You start to thumb through the cards. Global Express goes off to the side . . . you know that YTC Group is in a three year deal with your top competitor, so they're tossed over on top of Global. There's InterScope . . . you remember their purchasing director asked specifically about installation timelines . . . so he gets a separate spot on your desk. The buyer from Riddick Industries is new so that relationship barrier you've had there might be mitigated . . . place that with InterScope. Rachel subtly mentioned that her bosses at Axis were looking at Central America as the next expansion target . . . we have tremendous distribution channels down there . . . you need more information from Rachel on how to proceed. Four cards from Genesis . . . you remember those guys but you don't know anything about the company . . . you'll get your intern to do a little digging here. Oh, and here is the guy from the transportation division that your buyer, John, at Watkins has been talking about . . . that's perfect because you're on John's schedule for Wednesday already.

Your mindset has changed again. The stack of cards has changed again. Now it's no longer one monolithic group of names and numbers. Each contact is a path, on which the first step is assessment. Each assessment must include an analysis of fit and feasibility. From there you can prioritize and plan next steps. For some, the next step is merely to abandon the path as quickly as possible. For others, the next step may be to begin a full sprint. For most, it will be a purposeful stride forward. There is ore here. But you must properly and patiently mine it in order to find gold.

Qualify

Once targets have been identified, they must be qualified. Qualifying a prospect means establishing whether a potential customer is both interested in purchasing your product or service and able to make the purchase decision with the requisite resources to transact. If you are going to consistently generate revenues in a cost-effective way, it's imperative that the targets in which you invest time and resources have both the desire and the capacity to buy your product or service. Traditional approaches to qualifying prospects have adopted the MAD criteria, requiring salespeople to ask the following questions:

- Is there **M**oney allocated to purchase the product or service? Without sufficient resources, a target can't be qualified.

- Does the target have the **A**uthority to make the purchasing decision? The funds may be available, but if the individual with whom you're interacting is not in a position to give an authoritative thumbs-up on the purchase decision, the target isn't qualified.

- Finally, does the target have the **D**esire to make the decision to purchase? Even if the money is there and the target is in a position to buy, in order to be qualified they must be convinced about the fit between their current and/or future needs and what you're selling.

Although the MAD model is widely used in many industries, the traditional model is simplistic, short-sighted, and high risk. Why? Because it does not incorporate the critical variables reflected in CAN modeling. Using the MAD approach to qualify targets doesn't tell you whether there is overlap with the parameters that you identified as being most critical to the maximization of CLV. Doing this requires a taking strategic approach to qualifying targets that involves a type of weighting process. Targets are ranked by their overall attractiveness according to the four criteria identified in the CAN modeling.

First, salespeople have to consider the *strategic alignment* between the target and their specific goals. This involves thinking about whether there are any intangible factors that contradict what appears to be a CAN fit.

- Does the target "feel" right?

- Are there any infrastructure or network factors that make the target less attractive?

In order to justify any significant investment in a target, it's essential that you consider and account for any intangible factors that might emerge. Doing this helps to ensure—or to at least strengthen the possibility of—strategic alignment.

Second, salespeople have to consider whether there are likely *entry or expansion constraints*. This is accomplished by asking the question:

- Are there any contractual or other nonscalable barriers associated with the target?

In light of the goal of *maximizing CLV*, it is important to think how the target is embedded within other market relationships that might ultimately serve to reduce the potential scope and range of products and services the target either can or will consume. As an end game, in order to achieve a high-velocity cylindrical funnel with maximized CLV, all current accounts must ultimately evolve into partnerships.

- Are there any limitations to CLV for which to account when ranking the potential (or value) of qualified targets?

Finally, specifically account for all *costs associated with acquiring* a customer by asking the question:

• Is the time, cost, or risk necessary to acquire a target too high?

Although a target's potential CLV might fit the parameters you specified, it is also possible that the resources that you would have to expend to secure that account may prove too costly in the short term. In this kind of situation, investing resources to capture the account could create vulnerabilities elsewhere, thereby diminishing the potential associated with other alternatives. When qualifying targets, it's important to account for a target's strategic fit and to rank targets according to their strategic fit as well.

Red Door: Qualify

The story is the same this week as it was last week. You've spent countless hours preparing for a sales call with McComb Industrial. You built a customized presentation on your new automated packing system, because you know that this sale will push you over your target number and secure your annual bonus. As you finish the presentation with Julie, the procurement manager, you ask the do-or-die question: "So, after the presentation . . . what are your thoughts on our system?" The woman across the table smiles at you, and says that she thinks it has real potential. She'll definitely communicate all the information you provided to her boss, who is the buyer, and asks if you can leave your material as she stands to shake hands. She assures you that they'll get back to you "in a few weeks" as she ushers you politely to the door. As you walk toward your rental car, that pit in your stomach starts to grow.

McComb Industrial is located in Tulsa, OK, and has been on your target list for several years. You've sent them almost literally tons of samples, written hundreds of e-mails, tried to connect via LinkedIn, called every phone number in the book, and even tried a couple of "drop-ins" all to get someone's attention. Based on the amount of time and money you've spent, this conversation just cost your firm in the ballpark of $10,000. It was just by sheer luck that you happened to come across Julie's contact information at the Las Vegas trade show six months ago. Steve, from TGI Electronics, which does a lot of the installation work on your packing systems, was telling you about a job he had done previously at McComb and he happened to have had Julie's business card. Julie returned your initial phone call and you knew that you had your foot in the door.

After multiple phone calls with Julie and a brief review of your proposal, you decided it was worth the trip to Tulsa. Julie was young and had only been in her position for 18 months. Julie had been very supportive in the discussions. She really didn't ask many questions or challenge you on pricing issues. Your initial read of the situation was that Julie was a go-getter and that she is trying to make a name for herself. After the meeting, it's clear that assumption was off base. Julie was not the decision-maker. Now your hours of work—and presentation materials—are about to be communicated to the decision-maker; but by Julie, instead of you. You were so excited about the meeting you failed to qualify her as the decision-maker. You know that your offering is not the most competitive on price, so it's critical that you be there to present the real value message, and link it to McComb's business outcomes and goals.

The door is closing. Just as Julie starts to say goodbye, you stop and turn to her. You realize that this may very well be the last chance you have to get in front of the right people. You ask Julie who else is likely to see the proposal. When she says that Jim Stevens from Finance and Susan Smith (her immediate boss) actually have the final say, you start to get excited. Now you know who the players are. This may have been a tough lesson to learn, but there's still a chance to get the deal done. You offer to Julie that you're in town today and tomorrow. You can reschedule your flight. If there's a chance to meet with Jim and Susan, you'd love the opportunity to present to them directly. She calls in their office coordinator, and schedules a second meeting for the following day.

Personify

Once targets have been qualified, it is time to personify them. Personifying a target involves identifying the right person(s) within the target company—the points of contact for generating and increasing revenues. It is through the personification process that traditional sources such as referrals, networking, and trade organizations make sense. However, this only makes sense if you follow a systematic process to evaluate potential targets by using the CAN modeling approach and strategically ranking qualified targets. Leveraging widely available technologies such as Google, LinkedIn, social media, and databases is also useful when personifying targets, but only when strategic search mechanics are effectively used. When used properly, these technologies can reduce the diameter of the funnel by increasing the sophistication of targeting personification. However, using these technologies without following a disciplined sourcing approach does nothing to narrow the diameter of the sales funnel.

Target personification requires that you map a path to decision-makers that leverages the target's culture and hierarchy. The people for whom we tend to look when personifying targets occupy positions along the path connecting boundary spanners to decision-makers. Gatekeepers represent one such role. Their role is to function as a barrier between external constituents and decision-makers, and thereby insulate these individuals from secondary stakeholders such as salespeople. Along this path, you are also likely to find both potential users of your product or services and influencers who understand the target's culture and how these are likely to impact your offering within the target. Further along the path to the decision-maker are buyers whose role it is to acquire new products and services, again, subject to the feedback of influencers within the target. Finally, only after surpassing all of these role-holders will a salesperson actually encounter a decision-maker with the institutional wherewithal to define and to generate a firm purchasing contract. It is critical to understand how each of these roles are intended to shape the nature of the interactions that internal constituents (such as gatekeepers) have with external constituents (such as salespeople). Often, too much is made of gatekeepers as a sales obstacle. It is easy to fall into the trap of viewing gatekeepers as obstacles there to impede your progress along the path to target decision-makers. It is better to view them as simply another potential "advocate" for you and the value your products and services represent for the focal target.

These individuals, potentially including buyers, influencers, and users, constitute a *buying center*. A buying center is a group of target organizational members that has responsibility for making and finalizing purchasing decisions. When purchasing decisions involve significant resources, organizations often use buying centers as a way to incorporate the input and perspectives of a number of different organizational constituents. It's important to understand that the formalization of buying centers varies from organization to organization. They range from an informal ad hoc group to a formally sanctioned organizational body with established purchasing criteria and protocols. Developing an understanding of the organizational culture of the target can help salespeople to approach the personification process with tactical sophistication, and therefore increase the likelihood of achieving a positive outcome from the sales interaction.

Buying Center

The personification process that we outline above is called contact mapping. To successfully map out your prospect, there are several steps to follow:

- List all the individuals with whom you interact from the prospect company.

- List any other individuals at the company of whom you are aware or have heard of.

- Identify each of their roles in the company:
  - Gatekeeper
  - Influencer
  - User
  - Buyer
  - Decision-maker

- Create a map on how to navigate these individuals at the company. Consider which areas of value and risk each place on the map will address. This will be very useful when we get ready to build our value message.

Buying centers include *gatekeepers*, who are boundary spanners responsible for making the decision whether to move forward with a sales call prior to engagement of any additional organizational members. *Influencers* have a specific set of skills or expertise that influences purchasing decisions. These individuals typically have hands-on knowledge about the offering. *Users* are the individuals most likely to actually use the offering, and play a primary role in its installation, use, and dissemination. Although the role played by users tends to be overlooked, they are critical to the sales process, as they often have a great deal of practical knowledge that can be leveraged to advance the sales process. *Buyers* bring together and manage information flow and purchasing arrangements. Finally, *decision-makers* are the final arbiter responsible, ultimately, for making the decision whether to purchase an offering.

Call to Action: A Systematic Approach to Sourcing

Sourcing new prospects and lead generation is one of the most challenging activities a salesperson has responsibility for. It is time consuming, full of rejection, and one of the most tiresome tasks we're faced with. Unfortunately the success of our entire pipeline and sales funnel hinges on the quality and quantity of prospects that we generate. We challenge you to take a step back from your current lead generation method and to take a more systematic, process-oriented approach to generating prospects. Take a few minutes and develop a lead list based on the C-Squared method. Once you've created this list of (1) current customers, (2) customer's competitors, and (3) competitors' customers, prioritize them based on their similarities with your ideal customer profile. Now that you have a prioritized list that aligns with the necessary qualifications for a potential sale, start approaching these prospects from the best to the worst. Realize that building a strategic qualification list will require an initial short-term investment, but it will deliver substantial long-term financial payoff.

Chapter 3

Becoming a Knowledge Broker

"If you want to be happy, set a goal that commands your thoughts, liberates your energy, and inspires your hopes."

—Andrew Carnegie

Bridgette was worried about keeping her job. Pete hadn't prepared for their sales meeting with the second biggest account on their books. "We'll be fine, Bridge—don't worry" he had said. "How much could their requirements have changed in the last six months? We've got this in the bag. Don't worry. I've done this a thousand times. . . ." Walking into the meeting, Bridgette had a sinking feeling. She'd seen Pete operate, and he could definitely sling it. But the client had had some major turnover during the last quarter, and she wasn't sure that it would be "business as usual" with their new decision group. As soon as they opened the door, she knew they were done. Instead of the old, informal crowd they'd worked with for years, in front of them was a group of very young, very serious, business-school suits with iPads and calculators out, and not a smile between them. Pete bombed with his first joke, and it was all downhill from there. Now she was listening through the door as Pete got torn up by Frank, their sales manager, and she was next. If you fail to plan . . . plan to fail. . . .

THE PURPOSE OF THIS CHAPTER is to introduce a systematic process to help you take control of the sales process. Salespeople are historically notorious for "winging" sales presentations. Traditional planning typically relied upon the sales funnel and some predetermined conversion rate to set goals or forecasts—which is essentially an uncertain, unsystematic numbers game. But today's salespeople face a set of new challenges that make this approach much less effective. These challenges include everything from greater internal expectations and market turbulence to the increased power of customers given advances in technology, big data, and complexities of channels and buying centers.

There has never been greater need for salespeople to prepare and develop what we call "intuitive market orientation," which is based on extensive, precise research and market understanding prior to ever getting into a room with a prospective target.

Your ability and credibility as a salesperson is dependent on developing a customized sales plan that is centered on becoming an authoritative and informed source of information. This will allow you to develop strong, focused messages tailored directly to your target's obvious and unspoken current and potential future needs and position you to maintain control of the sales process.

In this chapter we will introduce the mechanics of the strategic sales process. We will address goal-related drivers underlying PLAN success, as well as the customer decision-making process—while emphasizing value creation, internal, and customer-related factors.

We will also focus on the ways to leverage information regarding customers, competitors, and the industry, and conclude with immediate next steps to improve your control of the sales process and become a knowledge broker to your customers and team members.[1]

The Strategic Sales Process

As we see in Figure 3.1, the way markets function is changing faster today than at any time in the past, and bringing with it the need to fundamentally rethink the sales process and the salesperson's role within it.

Figure 3.1. Changes in Selling Strategy

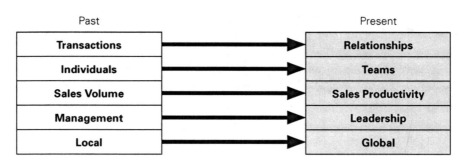

In the past, the primary emphasis was on:

- Transactions and increasing transaction volume
- Simple products and straightforward product lines
- Individual salespeople
- Sales volume, with a focus on numbers
- Account management and transactional processes
- Serving local accounts within simple geographic boundaries

Today, however, the emphasis is placed on:

- Sales teams capable of dealing with complex products and product lines.

- Building and developing long-term consulting or coaching relationships with partners, or other high volume customers.

- Sales leadership.

- Finding new and innovative ways to serve partners' current and future needs.

- Serving global customers within a broader, global context.

These changes in strategy have forced us to make significant modifications to the way we plan and sell. The strategic sales process begins with focused, tactical sourcing and a deep understanding of the customer and competitive environment as determined by CAN modeling. The CAN model involves identifying an ideal customer target profile by assessing the Characteristics, Activities, and Needs of the target, then assessing that customer's potential lifetime value (CLV), which is the value of the net profit earned from a customer during their time as a customer with you. These two processes combined help us develop criteria for selecting targets and opportunities.

After identifying an "appropriate" target, the next step in the strategic sales process is the creation of goals for the prospect. Sophisticated goals, which we'll discuss in detail later in this chapter, are tied directly to a specific set of desired measurable outcomes and key goal targets. Once goals and targets have been defined, and benchmarks for their accomplishment determined, you must define the best means to achieve these goals by creating a strategy—or "50,000-foot view"—toward goal accomplishment. Once the strategy has been established, the next step in the strategic planning cycle is to develop the tactical means or the operational steps necessary for achieving these goals. It is only after all of these strategic steps have been taken, and sufficient preemptive ground work has been covered, that you can justify the development of a proposal to capture a targeted prospect. This process becomes in many ways a cycle, because you want to continuously revisit both your goals and your progress toward their achievement prior to developing a proposal.

Proposal Objectives

The foundation of an effective, target-centered proposal rests on being intimately connected to your proposal objectives, and having a systematic approach toward planning and goal setting. Proposal objectives often are set or influenced by your company or manager. However, it's important that you are open to adjusting proposal objectives after completing the planning process, because conditions on the ground often require you to operate in a flexible way. Remember, these are proposal objectives, not CLV objectives. Be careful moving forward— everything you do from this point on has to be purposeful toward the achievement of these objectives.

	Steps for Success: Framing the Proposal
	Proposal objectives should always begin with asking five questions: What, Where, When, Who, and How.
1	Refer to the product in focus so factors including items, sizes, and flavors clearly reflect the *What* in your proposal.
2	*Where* addresses geography, so factors such as regions and in-store placements will be your focal landing zone in the proposal.
3	*When* captures issues related to launch—the dates, events, and promotions that are included in the proposal.
4	*Who* refers to the members of the buying center and understanding the roles that different individuals will play in the sales call.
5	*How* refers to issues such as price—what costs or margins constrain or bound your proposal objectives. As a general rule, successful proposals incorporate three to five specific sales or performance goals.

SMART Objectives

Sales goals refer to the specific levels of performance you hope to achieve. While they are often set at a tactical level in proposals, they originate from the strategic objectives of the company. Goals represent the outcomes and results that you expect to achieve as you move toward your most aspirational view of the future—these are the "What" items critical for the articulation of your vision. In order for sales goals to have the highest probability of success, they have to be SMART goals. The first step in SMART goal setting is to make your goals **S**pecific. For example, your proposal may focus on critical customer business drivers, such as increasing the prospect's operational and cost efficiency derived from your products or services—but that's too vague a goal to be effective. A more specific goal would be: "I will increase operational and cost efficiency 15 percent each quarter for the first three-quarters of the year."

Unless you assign a verifiable value to the increase for which you are striving, it will be difficult or impossible to understand whether you've been successful in accomplishing your proposed goal, or not.

This leads to our second SMART principle, which is that goals have to be **M**easurable. There needs to be some way to verify that the goal you've established (or proposed) has been met. You can measure whether you've been able to help a customer achieve an increase of 15 percent in operational and cost efficiency by examining quarterly cost records. Measuring how you are progressing on a goal by comparing it to a previous goal or measure will allow you not only to track progress, but to maintain focus on critical tactical and operational contingencies.

The goals you set also need to be **A**chievable. Proposing a goal that's too aggressive ("I will increase your operational and cost efficiency by 35 percent in the next month") can be discouraging and set up a classic "overpromise, underdeliver" scenario. Some coaches call these super-reach goals (We're going to win the regional tournament!), but if the goal can't be reached in light of the constraints that exist, then over time it becomes demotivating, and can be damaging to your reputation. So, keep your goals difficult, but attainable.

In order to be useful, goals also have to be Realistic, which means that your goals are consistent with other established priorities. If a goal like increasing operational and cost efficiency is consistent with other tactical goals, it won't detract from meeting other obligations and priorities. In fact, realistic goals can actually help you to reach other critical milestones rather than working against them. In contrast, goals like "successfully overhauling an entire IT infrastructure in conjunction with reconfiguring a top-to-bottom HR infrastructure" are probably unrealistic given practical product and service delivery limitations.

Finally, SMART goals need to be bound by specific Time horizons. There needs to be some identifiable end-point so your customer can see where you've taken them over a given period of time. "I will increase your operational and cost efficiency by 15 percent each quarter" is a good goal, because it provides a specifiable time frame for achievement.

Different types of goals typically emerge as you go about developing a proposal. These may relate to sales volume, profit, expenses, sales activities, or several of these in combination with one another. Different goal levels—goal difficulty—also come into focus as you begin to define the parameters of your proposal. The level of the goal selected can be based on many different factors, including sales history forecasts, company goals, conditions in the sales territory (customers' size, number, rate of growth, potential, etc.), impact on profitability, executive judgment, input from salespeople, or potential effects on salesperson motivation. As markets become more competitive, goal difficulty continues to increase. Although companies have reported an average 20 percent rise in sales goals, research shows that only 58 percent of salespeople are able to achieve their annual goals. This is partly due to the fact that goal achievement is increasingly a result of strategic effort and planning. The relationship between goal level and goal-focused effort typically follows an "inverted-U-shaped curve." In other words, people tend to dedicate the most effort toward goals that are moderately difficult, and less effort to goals that are "too easy" or "too hard." Sales managers must recognize that the most difficult or challenging goals should only be set for salespeople with the highest levels of confidence and ability. These are the salespeople most likely to thrive under the pressure of extreme "reach" goals.

Build the PLAN

In planning your proposal, your goals should not only be SMART, but also articulated clearly so you can track progress toward their achievement. Goals should be moderately difficult to motivate effort and to achieve wins that keep moving you forward. Goals need to be specific, but also flexible, especially when associated with customers. Once you start talking to the customer you may realize that the goals that sounded great on the drawing board are now out of alignment and need to be adjusted.

Finally, your plan should be built according to the PLAN principle. It should be:

- Purposeful and designed with specific parameters in focus. Not adopted or framed haphazardly.

- Driven by CAN modeling, and thus provide an opportunity to Leverage all available resources and take advantage of available synergies with current capabilities and economies of both scale and scope.

- Defined by Action, encompassing specific activities and actions.

- **Narrow.** A disciplined, well-conceived plan encompasses three to five SMART goals. This scope should enhance the probabilities of achieving successful outcomes.

Red Door: Getting Customer Goals Right

The customer goal is set. You have it all planned out in your mind, and written out with details, logistics, and specifics for delivery and implementation. All aspects of the plan fit in with everything you've been trying to do with this customer, and what you'd like to do moving forward. You're sitting in your car in the parking lot of TBR Printing. You take a few minutes to review your notes, and to get your head around the objectives for the day. The TBR account has been doing good, solid business with you for almost five months now. You're looking to upgrade your company's relationship with TBR to partner status, and this is the perfect day for the visit. Your regional manager is in town for the next two days. He's accompanying you on some of your sales calls for coaching and development purposes, and you also get the sense that you're being looked at for a promotion, which is something that your manager accidently let slip a couple of weeks earlier.

You figure this is a great account to call on. The buyer, Tom, is a pretty good friend of yours. He's a "sure thing," and will definitely reorder product from you, so that's a victory in and of itself. You also figure that this is a perfect opportunity to try and upsell Tom on the next level of the ink product in your portfolio. You've thought that you might also try to bundle the upsell with the additional extended service package offered by your firm. All in all, this would be a great piece of business, and would really help move you closer to your quarterly percent of quota. If what your manager told you is right, this could also mean a promotion for you as well. You've done your homework. You've dotted all the *i*'s and crossed the *t*'s and you're ready to make some money.

As you walk through these goals with your manager Steve, he asks, "So, how exactly will these improvements in product and service that you've got in mind for TBR at this point affect the end customer?" Your initial response to his question is, "Where is this question coming from?" You've just told him your well-developed, well-laid-out plan to generate, essentially, a 120 percent increase in business from this customer. You've shown initiative and creativity, and you're planning to meet needs the customer hasn't even recognized yet. But, you get the feeling that instead of the kudos you'd expected for the plan you've laid out, you're getting flack. Why?

Steve's been around a long time and he's been successful in a lot of businesses. He's a producer and he knows how to sell product and how to make money. What he's really asking you to think about—to recognize in light of the goals that you've laid out—is that it's important to consider the customer's customer.

You've got a good plan laid out, but understanding your customer's goals enables you to create new value propositions, and link these to specific business outcomes. So you walk Steve step by step through Tom's business. You go through his important goals and outcomes. Tom has said to you on multiple occasions that for him, delivering the highest quality product to his customers, on time, is of the utmost importance to him—that's where his critical outcomes are.

Steve isn't just there to watch you upsell in a vacuum, feeding you for a day. He doesn't want to give you fish, and watch you go hungry. He wants to help you learn how to fish on your own. Steve has helped you to recognize that, in the end, the way to transform customers into partners is in helping them to satisfy their own customers—satisfying the customer's customer is going to feed you for a lifetime.

Understanding the Customer Decision-Making Process

It is becoming abundantly clear to everyone involved in sales today that the nature of the sales process and critical sales-related activities are becoming increasingly complex. However, one thing hasn't changed throughout history—the interpersonal nature of selling. Whether it is a "simple" over-the-counter retail sale of a pack of gum, or an all-encompassing, long-term B-to-B sales solution stretching over years and across multiple business units, ultimately it's all about people. Within the salesperson-customer "dyad" there are always two parties involved in the interaction, but salespeople often neglect the other half of the dyad—the customer. As you go through your approach, what are they thinking? What does their decision-making process look like? In this section, we will explore a series of predictable phases involved in the customer decision-making process.

Knowing where your customer is in this process at any given point in time positions you to advance your proposal in a tactical way that builds on, rather than interferes with, the natural rhythm of a customer's decision-making process. As we see in Figure 3.2, this process is cyclical and provides a natural framework for advancing the conversation.

Figure 3.2. Customer Decision-Making Process

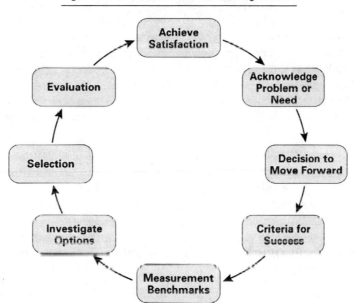

Jolles, R. (1999) *Customer Centered Selling: Eight Steps to Success from the World's Best Sales Force.* SimonandSchuster.com.

The first step is to have the customer acknowledge that everything isn't perfect. It is at this point that a prospect is created. Research suggests that 79 percent of people are in this stage of disenchantment, but that they tend to remain there unless prodded to articulate their dissatisfaction. There may be ongoing or nagging problems that impede them in making a decision. This is the pivotal phase of the decision cycle—getting customers to move beyond acknowledgement to actively reaching toward a solution.

The next phase involves resolving to fix the problem. This is a not a decision to buy your product or your competitor's product, it's simply a decision to act, and it typically emerges from one of two major causes. Either a single, major traumatic event tips the scales toward action, or many small problems finally accumulate to become a big problem that can't be ignored any longer. Most prospects are afraid to fix their problem.

In the next phase of the process, prospects try to establish the specifications of the problem—determining its dimensions and parameters and scope. The nature and parameters of the problem shape the solution. Customers make decisions based on needs, wants, problems, desired solutions, and a mix of everything. That means many times the criteria set by the customer may not be the best criteria to use. This means we need to help in reframing the issue. Defining the boundaries of the problem moves the decision from a vague, general sense of "something" needs to be done to a specific "this" needs to be done frame of mind. Determining the specifics surrounding the problem in this way typically reduces or eliminates the potential for disputes between buyers and sellers.

After they have established the problem scope, buyers start to evaluate alternatives based on the specifics of the problem they've identified. It is at this point that it is possible to begin to establish trust, and performance metrics for anticipated possible solutions. The customer will evaluate each product against each criterion, and verify their progress against benchmarks in the marketplace.

Following the investigation phase, customers have to make a selection, which is an emotional phase of the cycle. Once buyers make a decision, they tend to look for immediate results. This can be a problem because their emotions can blind them to inherent time lags often required for implementation outcomes. It is imperative that salespeople manage these expectations to enhance CLV. While customers often feel a sense of relief after making the decision, it is also common that they begin to feel anxious over perceived risks associated with having made the decision.

Finally, customers enter the evaluation phase. During this phase, they often experience buyer's remorse in light of inevitably closed-off "other" options. They will tend to feel discomfort as they balance conflicting beliefs about what they've done—relief at having made a decision coupled with uncertainty about whether it was the "right" decision.[2] They tend to make comparisons to available performance metrics and seek feedback from others to get confirmation that their judgment and decision-making were sound. It is important here to note that 25 percent of customers report that they would have made the decision differently, which bears on the potential for maximizing CLV.

Red Door: Customer Decision-Making

You're in the middle of chasing down a lead at TriTech that you got indirectly from a supplier who did work for them, when a customer calls and asks for an RFP (request for proposal). You've already got a good amount of business with this customer—almost a partner—and they're asking for a proposal on a set of ancillaries that would represent a substantial increase in their value to your company. You are immediately excited about increasing their value. You get a meeting with them to outline the scope of the project that they've got in mind. You feel pretty good about the meeting. You know that you've got the best product/solution currently available on the market. You're confident that you can deliver the solution that they're looking for at a competitive price, particularly given the relationship you've already got and your strong track record over the last several years. You go to meet the customer with high hopes and determination to convert this opportunity. Once you arrive at your customer's office, you find out that she is already more than half-way through the decision-making cycle. This is a serious RFP.

continues

She's determined the need, she's set the criteria required for the solution, and she's already started to solicit vendors to meet their needs in the near—and possibly intermediate—term. It all looks really good until you realize that there's a problem. The problem is that she set the wrong criteria. You've dealt with this exact same, recurrent issue at 10 other companies. You understand all of the dynamics and constraints involved in the implementation she'd like to see. You've seen the process from start to finish numerous times. Because of your experience, you know that the criteria that she's set to solve the problem are neither the most effective nor efficient solution to the problem. You've done it this way in the past, before newer solutions became available, and there are always expensive consequences associated with it. You've got a dilemma. Do you customize your offering in order to meet her invalid selection criteria so you get the business, or do you try to get her to backtrack in the decision-making process and reevaluate her criteria? Getting her to back up is going to be much more difficult, because of all of the capital (social and material) that's already been put into moving the decision-making cycle to this point. It's hard to make the decision to pull the trigger, and once it's been made it's hard to pull back from it. But, the other issue is that while everyone wants customization and customized solutions, nobody wants to pay for it. Whether you'll be able to afford the business is questionable. Your out-of-the-box solution is a value driver for your company, but once it becomes a customized solution the value proposition is more up in the air.

The question is, how do you get her to backtrack and make the right decision—for her company and for yours? You can explain your experiences with other clients and shock her with the level of knowledge and experience you've got. The technical insight you have into this particular problem is a competitive advantage. Share your success stories with her and help her to understand the latent issues that aren't likely to be as immediately apparent to her. Share your horror stories as well—carefully. Help her to understand the consequences of the misspecification in criteria that she's likely to face in light of her current positioning. Be an advisor—be a coach—and help her to make the right decision for her company. Help her to understand why in the end your expertise and knowledge will help her to both redefine her criteria more correctly and also to address her needs most effectively.

Value Creation

In the process of planning and developing a proposal, your proposal must speak directly to how your solution will benefit the customer, framed around helping them meet their goals—both personal and professional. This is the concept of *value*—or more accurately *perceived* value—which can only be defined by the customer. Although you may see your proposal as creating value, the customer is the only—and final—judge of whether you've been able to create value, or not. Beyond price, what are you providing the customer? As the market place becomes increasingly competitive, it is no longer enough to compete on a price basis. Value creation that extends beyond considerations of price has to be generated, framed appropriately, and communicated effectively in your proposal. In order for your proposal to truly create value, it must:

- Offer a clear path toward the most extreme, positive outcomes for the customer.

- Generate certainty for the customer (or as much certainty as it is possible to generate in this context) that your proposal provides the best solution in response to the problems they've identified.

- Be transparent so customers understand the process and implementation if agreement is reached.

- Reflect the customer's needs, goals, wants, and business outcomes.

- Explain how it benefits the customer's customer.
- Encompass implementation methodology, as well as value-increasing tactics to facilitate the customer's achievement of the value that they expect from your proposal frame.

Internal Analysis

At this point you might be feeling fairly confident you can deploy an effective proposal and deliver on prospects' or customers' emergent expectations. It is specific, measurable, and addresses key issues and business outcomes. But, have we taken measures to understand our *own* firm, particularly how we will navigate and work with internal teams to deliver on our promise? Here are a few questions to ask:

- How well do you know your company's history and vision?
- Do you know your own competitive position in the industry?
- How well can you navigate the internal structure of your own firm?
- How well can you work within a sales team environment?

Given the increasingly sophisticated product and service offerings that define current—and that will continue to define future—markets, the sales team rather than the lone salesperson has become an operational fact of life in sales. Effectively navigating your firm's internal structure requires knowledge of how things work and who to go to for information.

A group represents two or more people with a common relationship, but who do not necessarily rely on one another or work together to achieve common goals. A team, in contrast, works together to achieve common objectives and members also rely on one another to achieve these objectives. While groups work independently to achieve independent goals, teams work interdependently to achieve a measure of collective performance.

While synergy between members has positive performance consequences within work teams, the consequences for work groups are generally neutral. In work teams members have both individual and mutual accountability as they strive toward collective goals, while in work groups members have only individual accountability. Finally, while the skills of work group members are typically random and varied, those of work team members should be complementary, with members relying on one another to achieve collective objectives.

We can see in this 50,000-foot view of team effectiveness (Figure 3.3) the relationship between inputs and their component actions and the performance outcomes within sales organizations:

Figure 3.3. Team Effectiveness: The Big Picture

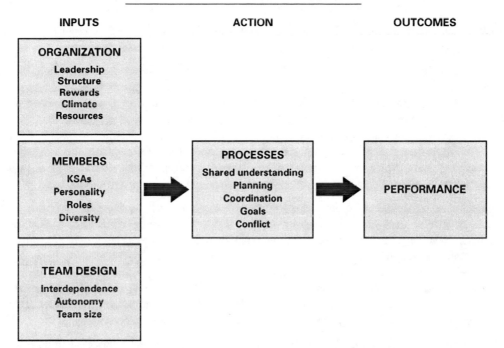

Within sales organizations, inputs trickle down to influence performance (outcomes) by going through a series of process transformations. An example of this is the emergence of a shared understanding between team and organizational members. By working together and experiencing many of the same things (leadership, policies, co-workers, norms, culture, customers, etc.) people tend to develop shared perceptions about what's required to effectively plan, coordinate, communicate, navigate interpersonal conflict, and achieve goals.

Successfully navigating these processes is critical for teams of salespeople responsible for an increasingly sophisticated set of products and services that exceed the scope of a single salesperson. Potential team performance can be thought of as a simple formula that totals up the synergies that arise among team members and contribute to performance (synergy) and the bottlenecks that impede performance.

Bottlenecks emerge when team members lack the KSAs—knowledge, skills, and abilities—required to accomplish goals, or when there's insufficient diversity to generate creative solutions to complex problems. Synergies emerge when members mentor and learn from one another, participate in ongoing professional development, and effectively leverage the advantages of their diversity. There are typically two types of diversity that characterize teams:

- Surface-level diversity
- Deep-level diversity

Surface-level diversity is based on things that we can see—age, race, ethnicity, and gender. Deep-level diversity is based on things that we can't see, like team members' experience, education, values, and personality. Bottlenecks like difficult tasks or teammate conflict often tend to occur because of surface-level differences in the early phases of a team's lifespan and because of deep-level differences later in a team's lifespan. However, teams can generate synergies by leveraging their diversity in terms of knowledge, perspectives, and experiences.

Synergies can improve problem-solving, innovation, and creativity. The key to generating performance benefits from synergies is being aware of diversity-related dynamics.

Remember, it takes time and effort to leverage diversity to help your team achieve its fullest performance potential. At the other end of the spectrum, similarity or homogeneity among team members can help the team to develop a shared understanding as members are "on the same page" regarding tasks, strategies, goals, roles, expectations, and timelines. This shared understanding can also help teams determine "who knows what" on their team. Bottlenecks can result when members have misunderstandings, deadline slippages, coordination breakdowns, or missed goals. Not knowing where knowledge and expertise resides within their team also can result in efforts being duplicated and team resources being leveraged inefficiently.

In contrast, synergies can emerge through effective and efficient coordination, common focus toward similar goals, and agreed-upon working styles. The way in which both formal (team leader, sales rep, sales support, etc.) and informal (controller, organizer, creator, etc.) team roles are navigated also has the potential to lead to either bottlenecks or synergies. Bottlenecks can emerge as a consequence of unclear role definitions or misunderstanding roles (both one's own as well as others'), unfulfilled team roles, and breakdowns in interdependencies. Synergies are more likely when the right people occupy the right roles, roles and interdependencies are well understood, and members' competencies and interdependencies are leveraged.

Team processes also can lead to either bottlenecks or synergies. Team processes tend to be of two distinct types:

1. *Task processes* — coordination, communication, planning, setting goals, and monitoring

2. *Team processes* — motivating, managing conflict, interpersonal relationships

Bottlenecks are likely to occur in the face of communication breakdowns (face to face or over e-mail), coordination breakdown, a failure to make or adjust plans, or as a consequence of interpersonal problems and conflicts. Synergies are most likely when members pause in order to make coherent and encompassing plans, rather than jumping right in without planning. Synergies are also more likely when members take time to reflect and assess progress and performance, and seek to learn lessons from both their successes and failures. Finally, synergies are more likely when teams explicitly address, rather than ignore, interpersonal issues.

Customer

We have talked about how customers make decisions, but it is also critical that salespeople systematically analyze and understand varied patterns of customer behavior. This knowledge provides insight into the type of interaction customers are likely to expect with salespeople, as well as their response to your proposal. Customers typically fall into four distinct style categories that are distinguishable by customers' levels of responsiveness and assertiveness.

The way people interact, or social style, tends to vary in a predictable way with regard to assertiveness and responsiveness. People with an *assertive* social style tend to be competitive, time sensitive, fast movers, quick decision-makers, and initiative takers. People with a *responsive social style* tend to be friendly, talkative, approachable, slower decision-makers, and more sensitive to others' feelings. Social styles depend on an interaction between assertiveness and responsiveness. As shown in Figure 3.4, social styles fall into four categories—amiable, expressive, analytical, and driver.

Figure 3.4. Attributes of Social Styles

	Low	**Responsiveness**	High
High	*Driver* • Demanding • Efficient • Decisive		*Expressive* • Enthusiastic • Dramatic • Inspiring
Low	*Analytical* • Persistent • Serious • Orderly		*Amiable* • Willing • Dependable • Personable

(Vertical axis label: Assertiveness)

Amiable Social Style

The amiable social style reflects a combination of low assertiveness and high responsiveness. Amiables tend to be the most receptive customers. They keep an office with a friendly atmosphere with pictures of their family proudly displayed. They hang personal mementos on the wall, and their desk is arranged to allow open contact with people. They also like solitary activities, but may wear casual or even flamboyant clothes.

Amiable customers typically want salespeople to show concern for them and for their problems. So, when interacting with an amiable customer, a salesperson should provide evidence depicting why the product is the best alternative to solve the customer's problem.

The meeting should be businesslike, and emphasize trust and friendliness.

Analytical Social Style

Customers who are low on assertiveness and low on responsiveness fall into the analytical category. They represent a category of customer that is more difficult to persuade. Analyticals often display achievement awards on the wall, and have a work-oriented office showing a great deal of activity. They tend to dress conservatively, and enjoy solitary activities such as reading or individual sports. These customers are typically seeking practical suggestions for ways in which to solve their problems.

Interactions with an analytical person should be approached with an eye toward the particular ways that the proposal addresses specific, identified problems. Salespeople should maintain an open, honest social atmosphere. They should retain a deliberate interview pace. They should also provide evidence demonstrating that they have systematically analyzed the customer's situation, and be explicit about how their offering can solve the problem. An analytic is interested in the salesperson's level of expertise.

Expressive Social Style

Persons falling into the expressive category are high on assertiveness as well as responsiveness. Expressives often reveal their social style by displaying motivational slogans on the walls of their friendly, open office. They tend to maintain a cluttered, unorganized desk, which is positioned for open contact with people. They may dress in a flamboyant way, and they tend to enjoy group activities, such as politics or team sports. Expressive customers often make decisions driven by their enthusiasm for the salesperson. Expressives prefer meetings to be quick and open, with a great deal of back and forth discussion.

Salespeople should provide expressives with evidence regarding who has used the offering in the past. Helping an expressive visualize the potential solution is important as they typically like competent, imaginative salespeople. There tends to be good potential for collaboration and importantly, partnerships, with expressives.

Driver Social Style

Finally, customers who are high in assertiveness and low in responsiveness fall into the driver category. Drivers often display achievement awards on their walls, but tend not to display posters or motivational slogans. Their offices prominently display calendars, and they position furniture so that contact with others occurs across their desk. They tend to dress conservatively, and tend to enjoy group activities.

These customers typically focus almost exclusively on achieving bottom-line results. A meeting with a driver has to be "all business." Drivers want to know how the offering will help them and the business succeed. When salespeople interact with drivers, the atmosphere should be businesslike, the interview pace should be quick, and the sales presentation should be explicit with regard to what the product can do. Drivers tend to have a more developed internally driven compass rather than a salesperson-driven compass.

Understanding customers' social styles plays a critical role in shaping your approach such that your proposal has the greatest probability of achieving success. It's human nature that we behave differently with different people, in different settings. Different people tend to see us in different ways. But, it's also important to remember that people have typical, recognizable social patterns and tendencies, or styles—how they like to interact with others—that emerge across social interactions. Although people are born with a certain social style, it can sometimes be influenced by things in your environment.

As a sales executive, recognizing and responding to social styles is an important skill. It's important to recognize that there are only a few styles that people tend to exhibit, and *most* people tend to display some identifiable behavioral clusters that you can label, anticipate, and prepare for prior to interacting with them. It's important to get "in synch" with others' styles. Because style differences can create friction, sales success requires that you be aware of these styles and develop the ability to adapt to another person's style. Successfully navigating these styles requires different approaches.[3]

Recognizing and Responding to Disparate Customer Social Styles

- Understand your own preferred communication style.
- Develop a greater understanding and appreciation for different styles.
- Manage relationships by adapting your style, or *style-flexing*.

Now, add another level of difficulty. Remember the buying center? In-depth knowledge of the buying center and its operational dynamics is critical for answering key questions that determine the likely success or failure of a sales proposal, including:

- Who makes the final decision?

- On whom does the approval of the project rely?

- Who benefits from your solution?

- What does the network of social relationships in the buying center look like?

- Who exerts social influence on whom, and what shape does this influence take?

- What's necessary to establish positive relationships with the "right" people in the buying center?

Depending on the culture and politics within the organization, the answer to these questions may not be straightforward; it's the salesperson's job to understand the interpersonal dynamics that drive these patterns. Answering these questions requires both an in-depth knowledge of the people with key roles in the buying center, and their relationships with one another.

Competitor

When it comes down to it, prospects ultimately make a decision to pursue either your offering or your competitor's offering. If you're going to be effective at value creation and differentiating the value creation mechanisms you propose, you have to be a sophisticated student of your competitors. When thinking about competitor analysis, can you answer the following?

- What are your competitors' core competencies?

- What are their offerings and benefits?

- Their prices?

- Their weaknesses?

- Their future plans?

- How would you sell against your competition when their bill rates are extremely low?

- How would you position soft and hard costs related to these things?

This type of analysis is called *competitor mapping*, which is about going through a process of seeing the attack before it comes. Traditional competitive analysis, which rests on fundamental assumptions that relate back to the sales funnel model, includes comparisons on the basis of features, service, and *price*!

In comparison to traditional competitive analysis, strategic competitive analysis is better aligned with the outcomes of CAN modeling, and includes comparisons based on where you can create greater value.

Figure 3.5. Value Creation

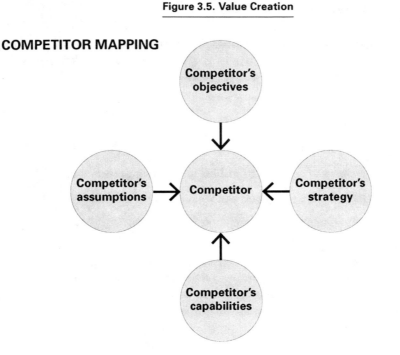

COMPETITOR MAPPING

This aspect of value creation is about *seeing the attack*.

As we see in Figure 3.5, developing a solid understanding of your competitors requires that you consider holistically the assumptions the competitor makes, as well as their objectives, strategy, and capabilities. Fundamentally, your competitors operate within limits defined by their internal strengths and weaknesses and their external opportunities and threats. Their strengths will tend to be featured in their proposal or offerings to your prospect. Their weaknesses will determine what they will tend to avoid in their proposal. Their opportunities will provide insight into their future plans, while their threats will yield insight into their concerns.

For prospects, who carry both heavy goals as well as heavy risks, it's essential that you engage in extensive competitive mapping—to make the kill. For accounts who have a heavy competitive standing, but who are only engaged along a limited number of vectors, you should engage in heavy competitive mapping and place a strong emphasis on environmental factors. For partners, who are engaged along multiple vectors in a long-term, high-CLV relationship, with heavy current business and products, it is critical to engage in extensive environmental mapping.

Industry

Throughout this chapter we have referenced "markets" and environmental impacts recognizing that our customers and competitors operate in an industry context that shapes the nature of how they view perceived value. This recognition must also become part of your view as you develop messages and value propositions for customers. Assessing the requirements and trends of a particular market or industry should inform key success factors you are positioned to provide, as well as those offerings your competitors might generate effectively.

We live in a digital world, with vast information resources that can be useful to us. Add to these the many proprietary research and analyst reports available in most corporations, and it becomes easier than ever to become "knowledgeable" about key industry trends and issues. When thinking about the industry in which you, your products and services, and those offered by your competitor are embedded, it's important to test your understanding of the following:

- Consumer trends
- Upcoming governmental or environmental regulations
- Global perspective on the industry
- Emerging technological advances
- Changes in the supply chain
- Customer's competitive standing in the industry
- Competitive trends in the industry

Consumer trends define the time horizon of your current offerings. They also represent a way to achieve the best approach to framing the value of currently available products and services. Your ability to predict potential roadblocks and constraints on the usefulness and value of current offerings or operating procedures can offset potential losses or service failures triggered by unanticipated changes in the market. This kind of foresight also can position you to take advantage of unprepared competitors.

As Napoleon Bonaparte famously stated, "Never interrupt your enemy when he is making a mistake." Anticipating the consequences of looming operational constraints positions you to do exactly this. A broad, geographically encompassing awareness of the shape of your industry is critical in light of emerging global trends and international supply chains. Being competent and retaining a strong, operational working knowledge of the intersection between your products and services and technology is merely a rudimentary starting point to operating effectively as a salesperson today. *Everybody* has to be a "computer guy" today. If you cannot speak confidently and with expertise about the vertical flow of materials underlying your offerings, it will be impossible for you to provide prospects any comfort that you can deliver the products or services you propose. In order to become the "only" option—or at least make the short list of options—on a prospect's or a customer's radar you have to know the game that they're playing, and also how well they're playing it. It is vital to know the difference between rumor and actual environmental conditions, so that your tactical dispositions coincide with actual market conditions, and your scarce resources aren't wasted in pursuit of red herrings.

Red Door: Customer Power

When Arthur Miller wrote his Pulitzer Prize–winning play *Death of a Salesman* in the late 1940s, it was at what might be thought of as the infancy of the age of technology in which we currently live. In 1949, NATO was founded, the first Polaroid camera was sold, the first automatic street lights were installed, and the first commercially available computer—the Manchester Electronic Computer—was released. When *Death of a Salesman* was written, notwithstanding the technological context surrounding its conception, in some cosmic way it must have been a prescient, Nostradamus-like prophesy of the emergence of the Internet. The Internet—and the democratic transparency that its nature and character represent, creates a substantial hurdle for the sales profession.

You've just gone on another sales call and had a terrible meeting. Another potential customer knew so much more about the products and services widely available to address their needs than you could have thought possible. You're really not sure if your prospects are looking on the Internet, reading reviews, talking to other suppliers, or all of the above. They're probably engaging in all of these information-gathering activities, and many more, that you haven't even thought of. The surfeit of information available from all of these sources is coupled with the fact that while young buyers think you're old and out-of-touch, old buyers think that you're too young and inexperienced and couldn't possibly understand their business. As they all like to say, to you and anyone who'll listen— "my business is different." The problem is that you've heard the exact same refrain from the past five prospects, all of whom have nearly identical businesses with almost identical challenges and opportunities. You're left with the recurrent question: In light of all of the information available on the Internet, how can you possibly add value?

You feel like you're becoming obsolete. Customers don't really need you any more—or don't think that they do. How can you differentiate yourself and make yourself indispensable in the sales process? How do you make your role compelling, again, and establish the critical value that you bring to the transactions that define success or failure in your world?

This is exactly where industry and environmental knowledge can differentiate you, making you invaluable to both your company and to prospects/customers. You can position yourself or your team as translators of technical information and knowledge, particularly as "solutions" become increasingly complex and multifaceted. Your expertise allows you to contextualize a wide range of options in ways that the Internet—or other information warehouses—cannot. The experience and insight that comes through years of working with a wide range of clients, products, and solutions enables you to play the role of coach or advisor, which is increasingly valuable in a world where an understanding of the implications of a particular decision is elusive.

Customers and partners don't have your tacit insight or understanding. The same sources of information out there—an information glut in many instances—can be useless to prospects and current customers that have no sense of what it all means for their business or how they can use it. They don't know how to contrast available alternatives because technical differences in what's potentially available aren't immediately apparent or interpretable. The sales role is changing—from a product mover to a partner coach. You are more than a conduit for your company's products and services. Your role is to become the guide in an increasingly complex and technologically sophisticated world. We'll talk more about this in Chapters 6 and 7.

Leveraging Knowledge for Insight

Simply generating knowledge about the attributes of customers, competitors, the industry, and your own organization in a vacuum does nothing to advance your sales, service, or value goals at all. Rather, it's how you *use* the knowledge that you have generated within the processes we've discussed that allows you to increase CLV and achieve competitive advantage in your industry. Adopting a sophisticated approach toward generating and applying the kind of knowledge we discussed in this chapter has an important effect—it allows you and your team to generate perspective and insight for and about potential customers that represent key points of differentiation between you and your competition. This will help customers develop the perception that you are an expert, prompting them to enter the decision-making process early, speed progress along that, and increase the chances that you will participate as they establish decision and selection criteria.

Call to Action: Enhancing Your Value Proposition

In closing, this chapter makes the case that research, information, and knowledge are especially important to the sales process. Gaining valuable insight into your customers' strategy and operations is an essential step in establishing competitive advantage through customized messages and offerings tailored to maximizing co-creation of value. Toward that goal of gaining competitive advantage in the market, in this chapter we discussed several areas in which salespeople can differentiate their value propositions from those of competitors. Setting goals, understanding the customer decision-making process, identifying social styles, and reading competitors and the market are increasingly important salesperson responsibilities. We therefore issue a call to action for all salespeople to make learning more about their customers a top priority, and to spend time setting goals and objectives prior to drafting customer proposals. Gaining valuable field knowledge and doing the prescribed research will not only allow you to differentiate your product and service offerings, but to enhance the value that is created. Ask your customers about their strategies and needs. Learn about coming market changes. Identify where you can enhance your value proposition before your competitors or customers demand it. All salespeople should seek to embrace their role as knowledge broker.

Endnotes

1   Verbeke, W., Dietz, B., & Verwaal, E. (2011). Drivers of sales performance: a contemporary meta-analysis. Have salespeople become knowledge brokers? *Journal of the Academy of Marketing Science*, 39(3), 407–428.

2   Sheth, J. N., Mittal, B., & Newman, B. (1999). Consumer behavior and beyond. *NY: Harcourt Brace*.

3   Dion, P. A., & Notarantonio, E. M. (1992). Salesperson communication style: The neglected dimension in sales performance. *Journal of Business Communication*, 29(1), 63–77.

Chapter 4

Reason and Role —

Account Needs and Processes

"The aim of marketing is to know and understand the customer so well the product or service fits him and sells itself."

—Peter Drucker

Mike was good — really good—at moving product. He could sell ice in Alaska. He prided himself on being able to make personal connections. But the world is changing. TecCom, where he'd worked for 13 years, wasn't asking him to move computer hardware any more. They wanted him to move systems. Not out-of-the-box systems—but customer-specific "solutions." Mike was now being asked to advise and consult, and he didn't really know where to start. He was heading into a meeting with Delaware Controls' regional executives. He had a general sense of what they were all about—but no real technical understanding of their business or customers. When he walked in, there was only a minute or two for small talk—which he'd have expected to go on for at least half an hour. All of a sudden, Kim Yonata, DC's CIO, said to Mike, "So, we're having trouble with our Denver supplier's subsidiary inventory management system; what can your product do for us?" Mike not only couldn't answer the question, he had no idea what she was talking about. . . .

OUR PURPOSE IN THIS CHAPTER is to introduce a new way of thinking about account management—the allocation of resources to meet organizational goals. We'll focus on why we do it and how it helps. We'll compare conventional ideas of account management with more contemporary market realities. Whether you have recognized the changing dynamics of the sales process, or not, it is no longer enough to "move product" in isolation. This process has become both more strategic and tactical, and as a result it has to be systematically integrated into the broader goals of the organization itself—both on the supply side and the customer side. We'll therefore address the functional relationships underlying the tactical implementation of a focused sales approach, derived directly from organization-defined strategic orientation. This orientation requires a deep knowledge of your customers, their business, and their objectives. Our goal is to help you understand what is required to develop an explicit, disciplined approach to creating value for customers and accounts through a modern perspective of the mechanics of account management.

When you think about key accounts, it's important to keep in mind the Pareto[1] principle—specifically, in this context, that 80 percent of annual sales are likely to come from 20 percent of key accounts. Despite this widely accepted saying, our research shows that only about a third of sales-focused companies today believe that they actually know enough about key account clients to communicate their value proposition effectively. This leaves two-thirds in the dark! Incredibly, about half of companies believe that their strategic account management process is ineffective. Further, approximately 60 percent of companies say that training in strategic account management will help them to generate higher revenues, profits, or customer satisfaction. What this means is that even though the vast majority of revenues come from a relatively small percentage of key accounts, most companies don't have enough knowledge about their key accounts to approach them strategically. Neither do companies have the confidence that they have the knowledge to change programs designed to focus on this critical group of clients.

The key objective for this chapter is to present new ways of thinking about account management. We want to create greater clarity about the importance of approaching tactical allocation of critical organizational resources in a way that directly coincides with measurable organizational goals. We'll start by addressing the importance of account management in the contemporary market, and how this role has changed over time. We'll define key terms and develop the link between tactical implementation and organizational strategy and the role played by cross-functional integration in this process. We'll then provide technical insight into how this process emerges, and discuss account relationships and needs. Finally, we'll offer key, practical insights to help you generate a more adaptive, functional approach to account management.

Account Planning—Why Do We Do It?

At the end of the day, no matter how good the products or services you offer, unless your account plan coincides with the strategic objectives and priorities of your customers, ultimately their needs are unlikely to be met. Without direct systematic planning, you'll end up losing accounts to the competition. Having a mature, coherent understanding of your current and potential customers' business is essential for the development of effective and compelling offers. This type of deep, technical insight into who your customers are isn't a luxury, it's a necessity.

To acquire a precise fit between what you offer and what the customer needs is a prerequisite which can only emerge through a complete understanding of your customer—or prospect. This customized approach has become a baseline expectation from customers. In order to be competitive, you must understand the underlying drivers of buyers' concerns; and the purchasing realities defining their market position. Today's buyers are actively focused on both the critical contingencies within their own company and their entire supply chain network. The bar has been raised. To reach this new standard, your account management strategy has to change as well, or you risk becoming obsolete in your industry.

Analyzing the objectives of key accounts includes developing an understanding for the advantages and disadvantages associated with each account. This will help you to envision the ways in which your products/services empower potential clients, and how to exploit or minimize disadvantages. Only you can generate the role similar to a consultant or a position coach, providing your customer with a playbook that takes into consideration a wide range of contingencies that bear on enhancing your customers' business.

In this chapter we will focus on the consultative approach, and the processes that will help to develop insight into the competitive context. With this approach, you will be able to develop a deeper understanding of the ways in which what you have to offer can contribute, in specific measurable ways, to your customers' specific goals and success.

The New Role of Account Manager

To execute effectively within the constraints that characterize the new market reality requires a fundamental shift in how you think about account management. In a technical sense, account management reflects the tactical allocation of resources to meet organizational goals. This implies that account managers make decisions about tactical organizational resources. These types of resources usually include things like sales representatives (who source and service customers), customer service staff (who serve as an ongoing point of customer contact), products, production capacity, supply chain capacity, samples, price, promotion, time, talent, attention, and so on. Yes, these include many of the tools that contribute to your organization's bottom line.

Organizational goals have traditionally included objective performance metrics such as profit, revenue, cost, share, markets, and other "hard numbers" the organization tracks. Resources are deployed in the service of these performance metrics and are designed to measure the satisfaction of the needs of customers (or accounts). But in today's marketplace, customers may have differing capabilities, and suppliers may set different goals for each customer, dictating that resources and measurement are applied in conjunction with individual versus aggregate goals of customers.

Lastly, in the not too distant past, "information" was less readily available, making the natural ebb and flow within markets more stable. Under these circumstances, the activity set of the account manager role was comparable to that of a salesperson. Their responsibilities included sourcing customers, making transactions, and doing this over again and again. This traditional role has changed significantly given today's access to real-time data and information. Today, account management has become an entirely different process demanding a much wider and deeper activity set. Account management is no longer equivalent in function to the role of a salesperson. In fact, these two roles don't even remotely resemble one another today. In contemporary selling contexts, an account manager is more aptly equivalent to a *manager of profit*: orchestrating resources, information, and strategy to achieve organizational goals.

Tactical Implementation of a Strategic Approach

In today's more complex environment, sound account management strategy requires an understanding of corporate strategies—both internal and external. This includes the development of marketing plans complimenting the relationships that these strategies implicitly and explicitly encompass. Account managers today, like salespeople, have to source customers, but they also have to analyze customers in order to categorize them and develop effective, comprehensive, logical account plans. See Figure 4.1.

Figure 4.1. Categorizing Customers

Source customers → Analyze, categorize, and plan

Like the traditional salesperson role, account managers have to sell to accounts, but they also have to manage and source these accounts in a way that supports their company's strategic goals. They must take a "forest for the trees" perspective in all of their boundary-spanning client interactions.

Sell to accounts → Manage, support, align accounts with goals

Perhaps most challenging, in light of ever-increasing resource constraints, account managers today must lead teams of sales representatives and support personnel to close or manage business. These individuals play a critical role in maintaining and coordinating the vast amounts of complex, dynamic market and strategic intelligence that are central to effective account management execution.

One-on-one interaction → Lead, coordinate, and communicate in a team setting

The nature of this essential role is continuing to evolve alongside the ever more complex and competitive market contexts which define it.

Within account management, wherein resources are deployed in the pursuit of organizational goals, it is critical to think at two distinct levels or perspectives. Resource deployment is inherently a tactical reflection of organizational strategy. So the organizational perspective serves as a starting point for determining where, when, and how much of a particular resource to deploy in order to generate outcomes that match specified (strategic) levels of profit, revenue, market share, and so on. Because these resources are linked to organizational strategy, it is important to think strategically about their tactical implementation. Doing so increases the discipline associated with the administration of resources, as well as the probability that these deployments will actually yield outcomes that benefit the organization. As we see in Figure 4.2, it also is important to note that we think at a second level: applying the principles of account management to effective negotiation with customers and their needs. Account management principles are also easily transferable to product management, territory management, division management, and subsidiary management as well.

Figure 4.2. The New Role for Salespeople

All of these management domains maintain performance goals served by pools of organizational resources that have to be allocated tactically to achieve strategic measurable outcomes, and thus the importance is paramount throughout the organization at many levels.

The Importance of Coordination across Functional Departments

A critical aspect of the account management role that is emerging today concerns coordination of functions. Today's organizations often support team-based or cross-functional environments, which makes the coordination of functions across the company essential. While there are many good aspects of this interfunctional coordination, perhaps the most important is that account managers are responsible for the coordination of sales, developing among salespeople a consistent orientation toward the organization's product and service offerings. Communication is key. Making presentations across multiple departments helps to maintain a coherent cross-departmental understanding of the key aspects of critical accounts, their features, and their liabilities. Assigning strategic account goals helps to generate team awareness of essential performance criteria, and thus impose discipline in resource allocations deployed in the service of these performance expectations.

Account managers operate in numerous ways to enhance efficiency and effectiveness of resource utilization for the customer and firm. For example, when account managers establish buying procedures, they essentially develop standardized approaches, which can lead to economies of scale and even organization-wide transactional efficiencies. Measuring promotion effectiveness also increases the effectiveness of resource deployment and achievement of strategic goals. Determining pricing strategies helps encourage adherence to strategic goals and provides a clearly established reference point for resource decisions. Coordinating service, negotiating contracts, and managing account contribution are all examples of coordination within the cross-functional team environment that can increase the strength of the connection between thinking strategically and acting tactically.

Challenges and Account Management Response

While creating cross-functional integration is an essential element in achieving coherence in organization-wide resource deployment, this coordination is not without its challenges. As we note earlier, the nature of the game has changed in fundamental ways. Because computing capacity is both widely available and inexpensive, customers have access to more—and more complete—market and product information than ever before. This has shifted the balance of transactional control, substantially increasing the power customers wield in their negotiations with suppliers. Because suppliers no longer hold an advantage with regard to the availability of technical or market information, they have to address customer needs in light of this new reality. Their ace in the hole, so to speak, comes when customer engagement depends on suppliers' ability to customize their value propositions in ways that are unique and inimitable.

Although information is essentially available everywhere and to everyone, how suppliers use that information in conjunction with their own specific resources and capabilities remains a potential competitive advantage. In response to increased customer power, account managers are responsible for customizing value propositions in ways that the competition is unable to simulate in a cost-effective way.

In addition to increased customer power, organizations also face heightened competitiveness across virtually all industries. Profit potential is reduced in industries with lower barriers to entry by competing firms in similar markets, and cheaper substitute products. Profit potential also is challenged by consolidated competition. The heavy competitive pressure suppliers and purchasers are capable of levying today, can diminish both gross revenues and margins. In order to address these threats, account managers are responsible for moving salespeople away from progressively old-fashioned, ineffective, isolated sales approaches toward a stronger value-focused approach to selling. This helps to shift current and potential customers' decision-making burdens toward suppliers in the position to offer the highest value, not merely the lowest price—which as we highlighted earlier are not the same thing. It is critical to develop solutions of higher value.

In light of the combined influence of seemingly ever-increasing market competitiveness and an extended, intense cyclical economic downturn, many markets also are experiencing a serious—even grave—absence of growth. New accounts and legitimate prospects are fewer and farther between. It was only a few years ago when generating new business was a relatively straightforward, albeit difficult process—but this is no longer the case. In response to this general, almost unending belt tightening, account managers must seek avenues to generate growth in key accounts. To do so, however, requires deep insight into the functional contingencies of these Pareto-critical revenue generators. One consequence of the shift in focus toward deepened insight into the business critical imperatives of customers is that business volume must evolve into business value if organizations are going to survive. It is simply too uncertain a prospect—and too expensive an endeavor—to cultivate new accounts using conventional models. Account managers must seek growth in key accounts rather than merely seeking to grow account numbers.

To make matters more difficult, all of this change is happening within markets that are increasingly becoming mature and that therefore have limited profit potential. When the supply and demand of products and services begins to reach a balance, market forces lead to a state of price equilibrium wherein competition increases and profits fall. Because of the stagnation that accompanies market maturity, account managers are responsible for stimulating new markets for their products and services. This may take the form of creatively finding new applications for currently existing products and services, where offerings are marketed in new ways with an evolving functionality and spectrum of use. This also may take the form of broadening offerings vertically to generate front- and back-end services in support of current products. The critical responsibility is the adoption of creative approaches toward stimulation to avoid the cost consequences of maturing markets.

Finally, in specialized situations, account managers may also have to deal with the commoditization of their products and services and the downsizing that is appearing everywhere in response to marketing tightening. These challenges highlight the critical responsibility of account managers to generate product/services differentiation and apply resources toward organizational goals for the most value. Differentiation can help to reduce commoditization pressures, while a value-centered approach can highlight advantages otherwise obscured in tight markets. What is clear is that heightened competitiveness across all markets has led to a broadening of the responsibilities of account management.

Strategy Implementation and Facilitation

Given the importance of maintaining a disciplined, strategic approach, it is essential to understand that the direction of inertia in the implementation of these tactical decisions is downward. The direction of the resource allocation process is defined by the broad, organizational view that ultimately is serviced by these resources. As a matter of practice, account managers make resource decisions within an operational context shaped by their organization's strategy. However, this is not a one-way process. It is better thought of as a two-way process, where the account management process actually "trickles up" to influence organizational strategy development.

Figure 4.3 Account Manager Influence

Thus, the account manager actually contributes to both the upstream and downstream of the strategy hierarchy, which you can think of as a pyramid as we see in Figure 4.3. At the top of the pyramid is "corporate strategy" which serves as the ultimate point of departure for all resource-focused decision-making—what account managers "do" in the new world. Where resources ultimately go depends on strategy, and thus in a functional sense these decisions operate in the service of that strategy.

In the next level of this hierarchy is the marketing plan, which answers questions such as:

- What is the current business or economic environment?

- What opportunities or challenges are currently present?

- What business objectives have been established?

- What do you sell and to whom?

- What differentiates your products or services from competitors'?

- How will you communicate value to your customers?

- How is progress toward organizational goals or "success" ultimately measured?

A marketing plan also provides planning discipline to maintain strategic direction and facilitates communication with senior management and with other parts of the organization, as well as their buy-in on tactical direction in the service of organizational goals.

Implementation

At the bottom of the Figure 4.3 pyramid is the account manager. Although account managers appear at the bottom of the hierarchy, they represent the foundation of any organization and typically have the greatest impact on performance. In playing the implementation role, account managers operate across the spectrum of the strategic hierarchy, primarily executing corporate strategy at the account level. The implementation role involves a number of different activities which include:

- Understanding corporate strategy and derivative marketing plans.

- Communicating strategy to internal stakeholders and external customers, which helps to create the necessary buy-in for cohesive, coordinated, purposeful action.

- Sourcing customers and assessing the potential of prospective customers, which serves to increase pipeline efficiency and minimizes wasted resources, time, and effort.

- Developing account plans, managing accounts, and allocating resources in accordance with these plans.

Account managers also have to *sell*! In the implementation role, the importance of actually producing cannot be overstated. However, in light of the increasing complexity of the market in which selling occurs, account managers also must both create and manage teams with the collective capacity to execute in this context. Selling is no longer a pursuit that can be consistently successfully accomplished by one person. Account managers facilitate implementation through their role as performance evaluators—assessing and adjusting performance and performance metrics in accord with stipulated strategic vectors. Finally, account managers facilitate implementation by serving as a point of accountability in this process—being responsible for publicly established, quantifiable, strategic outcomes.

Facilitation

Although functionally acting as an instrument in the service of a broader set of essentially depersonalized strategic goals, account management does not merely expedite implementation of these goals—it facilitates these goals as well. The account management role functions as an "intelligent" process driving the collection and analysis of external data that ultimately may play a role in shaping the nature and direction of the organizational strategy. Account managers can exert influence on organizational strategy, broadly, through learning and communication with the upper echelons. Account managers, who are most directly in touch with extant operational context constraints, are in a position to gather and convey information regarding market conditions.

This kind of intelligent collection and dissemination should enable organizations to modify strategy to more directly account for current realities. Account managers are positioned to collect data reflecting customer preferences and share these data with the strategic-level executives within their organization. Being at the bleeding edge of customer intelligence ensures that company strategy will never be reflective of outdated transactional realities. The facilitation role also relies on account managers' understanding of their own organization's competitive positions. Although theory and practice should theoretically coincide, in practice their coincidence depends fundamentally on current competitive realities *and* awareness of current competitive position. Failure to maintain current market knowledge can create operational vulnerabilities that can be exploited by competitors occupying a superior market position. Account managers can help their organization avoid these traps by understanding the current state of the game.

Account managers should also play the facilitation role by being a source of innovation. Having a deep understanding of customers' critical contingencies and goals can help to ensure that current products and services are positioned, conventionally, in the most effective way possible. This insight can serve as a point of differentiation by allowing account managers to create new points of insertion through innovation that broadens the value that can be derived from these offerings in other words, finding new ways to frame the utility of available products and services, or new, innovative combinations. Account managers can enact their role as facilitators by developing and propelling individual salespeople into roles that most effectively utilize their full human capital potential. Occupying the space between the upper echelons and the on-the-ground implementation of organizational strategy, account managers are in an essentially unique position to serve as organizational talent scouts. These individuals understand where their organization is trying to go, they understand where their customers are trying to go, and they know the actors on both sides of the boundaries as they position who will play key parts in this process. Developing their own employees, and propelling talent in the right direction, can only increase competitive positioning.

Finally, as in their roles as implementers, account managers also can facilitate strategic goals by remaining a visible point of accountability on the horizon. In practice, the organization is an abstract entity, wherein employees' exchanges take place vis-à-vis "critical members"— frequently immediate supervisors, but also account managers—who deliver, interpret, and enforce policies and practices. Account managers essentially serve as the embodiment of the organization to employees. As key representatives of the organization, account managers shape employee attitudes, expectations, and experiences. As an embodiment of the organization in the abstract, they influence others' sense of responsibility, adherence to established practices, and dedication to the achievement of organizational goals—generating grass-roots buy-in and support.

Playing Both Sides of the Fence

Because of their unique perspective regarding both their own organization's strategic goals and resource base, and their insight into customers' operational realities and aspirations, account managers essentially become double agents, occupying multiple boundary-spanning roles simultaneously. These individuals have to constantly keep in mind multiple, quasi-objective perspectives concurrently, balancing what they know and what they communicate against what they have to refrain from disclosing or feel obligated to disclose—both internally and externally.

As boundary spanners, occupying a position that requires playing an "insider" role both within their organization and outside of it, account managers have enormous potential to weave close ties. From their own organization's perspective, they have to understand their customer's business—inside and out—as good as (or better than) at least some of the customer's own executive personnel. On the flip side, from the customer's perspective, the customer knows the supplier, and knows that the supplier knows the marketplace, and is positioned to make offerings that coincide with current on-the-ground realities. From the insight they've worked to develop, the organization is positioned to develop strategy to tap into the constraints implied by their customer's business model, and to build value to capture their business. From the customer's perspective, this ensures that the company has a unique understanding of their needs, and delivers value.

Finally, from their own organization's perspective, account managers ultimately are responsible for building brand equity with the customer in order to retain their business for the intermediate term. From the perspective of the customer, this facilitates leveraging of supplier capabilities to enhance their own business objectives. There is a constant navigation of both sides of the boundary that account managers span—potentially head-spinning—which brings with it correlated internal actions and external perceptions that ultimately determine whether business is likely to be retained or lost.

Multiple Personalities

In addition to occupying a role that bridges multiple organizational realities, account managers have to adopt multiple personalities to successfully inhabit their role. These personalities reflect the inherent complexities of the role bearing on the nature of their ongoing internal and external responsibilities. The multiple personalities are influenced by their interactions with multiple stakeholders and the expectations of both internal and external constituents, as well as interactions taking on both transactional and relational aspects as we see in Figure 4.4.

Figure 4.4. Multiple Personalities: Internal vs. External

Internal Responsibilities	External Responsibilities
Resource manager	Resource deliverer
Risk manager	Risk taker
Standardized strategy	Customized value
Internal salesperon	External salesperson
Marketplace knowledge	Supplier knowledge
Trusted face of account	Trusted face of supplier
Tireless worker	Tireless worker

While internally account managers are viewed by superiors and subordinates alike as a resource manager—or value manager—externally they are viewed as a resource deliverer. While internal stakeholders view account management as the allocation of scarce resources toward strategic goals, external stakeholders view this same endeavor as a delivery of scarce resources toward the creation of value—the same activity takes on distinct aspects of significance depending on the perspective from which it is viewed. While internally the account management role is synonymous with that of a risk manager, external stakeholders are more apt to view this individual as a risk-taker. While the embedded, contemporary process of familiarization with customers' business leads to the account management approach being viewed internally as standardized strategy, this roll-out is viewed by customers as a process of generating customized value.

It also is important to recognize that the political capital necessary to deploy resources in accordance with the execution of this approach requires the generation of buy-in from key internal stakeholders. As a consequence, account managers are likely to be viewed within their own organizations as internal salespersons. At the same time, as their active, explicit focus is on generating productive relationships externally, they are viewed, despite being embedded, as an external salesperson. Internally, account managers are viewed as having broad marketplace knowledge, while externally they are viewed as a source of supplier knowledge.

Within their own organizations they are acknowledged as the trusted face of a revenue-producing account, while externally they are viewed as the trusted face of a value-producing supplier. Both internally and externally—not surprisingly!—they adopt the role of tireless worker, simultaneously maintaining and deploying the architecture necessary to execute strategy, while continuing to update intelligence and knowledge stocks to keep that infrastructure from becoming obsolete.

Transactional vs. Relational Engagement

In addition to adopting a frame of reference consistent with a stakeholder position, account management requires a simultaneous maintenance and understanding of both transactional and relational patterns of engagement in the process of seeking to maximize customer lifetime value (CLV). As we learned earlier, CLV reflects the net profit earned from a particular customer during their tenure as a customer. Any particular account's estimated lifetime value influences the approach taken to prepare and perform the sales process—whether a transactional or a relationship focus is most profitably adopted.

A transactional focus is increasingly incompatible with the constraints of the hyper competitive market landscape, unless a partnership emerges (i.e., maximum CLV). It only reflects a single sale mentality. In contrast, a relationship focus—with an emphasis on expanded, next-level framing—implies a broader and deepened focus on CLV. In light of the costs and uncertainties associated with the generation of new business, the relationship or CLV focus is more conventionally consistent with the investments necessary to operationalize the modern account management role—more expertise and insight require a greater investment of time and resources.

There are key differences between a transactional focus and a relational focus. While a transactional focus will tend to highlight product features, a relational focus is reflective of a focus on customer needs. A transactional focus also highlights both a transactional, single point of contact while a relationship focus highlights continuous multiple, varied contacts. While a transactional focus highlights limited commitment, investment, and information sharing, a relationship focus highlights extensive commitment, investment, and information sharing.

Although there are clear points of advantage associated with both a transactional and relationship focus, the account management role requires effective navigation of these approaches to maximize CLV. This is of course the account manager's ultimate goal, which ultimately is best reflected in a relationship versus transactional focus.

Steps for Success: Transactional vs. Relational Approaches

We've been focused on the question of CLV throughout the book. This focus has been perhaps most directly relevant in consideration of the approach and tactical mindset to adopt within transactional versus relational interactions with customers. They are different, and require a different mindset.

Focus: At its core, while the transactional mindset emphasizes the *single sale*, the relational mindset emphasizes *Customer Lifetime Value*.

Emphasis: While the transactional mindset emphasizes features of the *product*, the relational mindset emphasizes *Customer Needs*.

Contact: While the transactional mindset emphasizes *intermittent* (transactional) contact with customers, the relational mindset emphasizes *Continuous Contact*.

Touch: While the transactional mindset emphasizes a *single* point of contact, the relational mindset emphasizes *Varied Points of Contact*.

Commitment: While the transactional mindset emphasizes *limited* commitment, the relational mindset emphasizes *Extensive Commitment*.

Investment: While the transactional mindset emphasizes *limited* investment, the relational mindset emphasizes *Extensive Investment*.

Information: While the transactional mindset emphasizes limited information sharing, the relational mindset emphasizes *Extensive Information Sharing*.

Nurturing Account Relationships and Understanding Needs

An established process underlying the maximization of account lifetime value begins with the acquisition of the customer—or prospecting. Accounts must be generated to become customers. Then increased revenues underlying account value may be derived by cross-selling or up-selling. Retaining these customers is essential. It also is essential to reduce recurring variable costs through the generation of economies of scale and scope. In order to achieve these outcomes it is vital to have developed a complete understanding of account relationships across four broad categories: basic relationships, cooperative relationships, interdependent relationships, and integrated relationships.

As with the strategy hierarchy we discussed earlier, these relationship types may be thought of conceptually as existing in a pyramid form. "Basic" relationships form the base of the pyramid (because these relationships are the most common of the four categories), with "integrated relationships" forming the smallest, and most potentially lucrative, category at the top of the pyramid.

Three initial steps are important in defining and evolving the account management relationship:

1. Understanding the nature of the current relationship with a client.

2. Determining how far the relationship "can" go.

3. Making a plan to move forward toward the type of relationship identified in step 2.

Account management begins with a foundational understanding of the nature of these relationships. As we mentioned, there are four types of relationships that influence how we approach and engage customers. These relationships are viewed in Figure 4.5.

Figure 4.5. The Four Types of Account Relationships

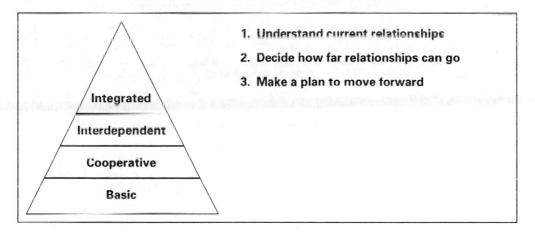

Basic relationships are the most common relationship pattern that emerges with clients, and are essentially transactional with an emphasis on efficiency. They tend to be driven by a cost frame, and consequently success in the relationship is measured by price. Basic relationships most frequently retain only a single channel of communication, with very little information sharing. Further, these relationships may be thought of as being reactive rather than proactive, where problems are allowed to emerge and are then dealt with in an ad hoc fashion. Basic relationships also tend to have a personal reward structure and are characterized by a standard, less complex account organization.

The next level above basic relationships is *cooperative* relationships. Here the selling company is perhaps (but not necessarily) a preferred provider but definitely has a more collaborative relationship with the account. Although the selling company adds value to cooperative relationships, exit from these relationships is not particularly difficult. Cooperative relationships tend to be characterized by multifunction contacts, although the relationship is still primarily with the buyer. The organization is fairly standard, with limited visits to the customer, limited information sharing, and only marginal feelings of mutual trust between the supplier and the customer.

Further up the pyramid are *interdependent* relationships. This is where both parties explicitly acknowledge the importance of the other. The supplier is a principal or sole supplier, and exit from the relationship is more difficult. The relationship is characterized by a larger spectrum of multifunctional contacts. The supplier has a deep understanding of the customer and the customer's business, and there is a great deal of explicit information exchanged within the context of regular, ongoing dialogue. Partners in the exchange engage in collective, proactive strategic planning, engage in joint innovation and development projects, and develop a growing level of trust in the relationship.

Finally, at the highest level of the relational pyramid are *integrated* account relationships. Here both parties in the exchange are mutually dependent on one another, with the supplier usually occupying a sole supplier role. As a consequence, these relationships have extremely high exit barriers. In an integrated relationship there are dedicated cross-functional teams, with open information sharing on all subjects and transparent costing systems. These relationships are characterized by mutual trustworthiness at all levels, where both parties are engaged in joint long-term strategic planning often with profit sharing structures in place.

The importance of understanding the characteristics of these account relationships is that they define the nature of the actions that suppliers take vis-à-vis their customers. This includes what level of resources to devote to the relationship, how many channels of communication to leave open, how much and what kinds of information to divulge, how to define success, and so on. If suppliers have an inaccurate sense of the degree of engagement accounts have invested in the relationship, this could lead to a potentially catastrophic misallocation of resources. It is critical to avoid what is known as "supplier delusion," where the supplier's view of the relationship is higher on the pyramid than the customer's view of the relationship. When these views are in synch with one another, both parties are left with a feeling of having engaged in productive interaction. Developing an accurate sense of the customer's view of the relationship and tying this view to operational decisions surrounding resource allocation is critical to avoid expensive consequences.

Change Your Approach and the Contract

Ultimately, a great deal of the potential utility of successful account management depends on how well you really know your key accounts, and how they in return view you—and most importantly, whether these views are compatible. As we've stressed throughout this discussion, it is essentially irrelevant how well you've developed your key account plans unless these plans fit with your customer's strategic goals and operational priorities. Unless there is a fit there, the development of the plan is really an academic exercise. Having a foundational understanding of your customer is critical in being able to adopt the "right" strategy and making what ultimately are acceptable offers to current and/or prospective accounts. Your objective is to understand what influences your buyer's concerns and the key aspects of the purchasing context you're operating in. Because buyers are in tune with the concerns of their organization, their supply chain networks, and the imperatives relationships imply, those become, by necessity, your concerns as well.

But, we are not done with our analysis yet. Now we must further identify our key accounts, as well as what relationships we hope to achieve, using strategic analysis to help ensure that these relationships are profitable and sustainable.

Here is a four-step process for the development of solutions that ultimately has the capacity to help us match-up successfully with customers' needs and strategic goals:

1. Registering on your customer's radar screen.

2. Developing an in-depth understanding of the customer and their operating environment.

3. Uncovering the customer's objective.

4. Developing solutions that align with these needs.

We address each of these four steps in sequence below.

Step 1: Developing Awareness (Registering with your Customer)

In order to break into the decision space that defines where your customers generate potential alternatives as to which suppliers to have meetings with, you have to become a part of their awareness set of suppliers—you've got to register on the radar. In college football recruiting, active scouts develop lists of top high school prospects from around the country. Unless a player has made it onto one or another of these lists, regardless of their talent level, most division I A schools won't even bother to take a look. Some schools won't look at a player who isn't on multiple lists. There's a reason for this. Making it onto one of these lists—being in the top 100 players in the country—is reflective of a vetting process that everyone in the game understands.

If a name isn't there, the assumption is that there's a reason for the omission—real or imagined. But, being on the list isn't the same has being awarded an athletic scholarship. It's merely a precursor—or perhaps more accurately a hurdle—toward consideration. There are signals that players give out, and that scouts detect, categorize, and weight in a systematic way, that typically serve as the basis for being vetted and included. Supplier consideration works much the same way. Suppliers also give out signals that are likely to get them noticed—to get them into a customers' awareness set.

Action Steps for Registering with Your Customer:
- Focus on product and service quality
- Optimize delivery time and price
- Master communication and proactivity

These are just a few of the perceptions that drive the wedge.

Step 2: Create a Knowledge Base
(Developing In-Depth Customer Understanding)

Through effective communication, you can demonstrate your processes for handling the relationship. You can also show how you will keep customers informed of any emergent or possible delivery issues. Proactive communication serves as a signal that you are thinking about improvement and that you are willing and able to move beyond the status quo to generate the highest possible value for the customer. Communication and proactivity differentiate the fast, strong, good-hands athletes who make the top 100 lists from those who don't make the list.

Once you've "made the list," the next step is acquiring an in-depth understanding of the customer environment and the customer drivers. A series of drivers play a primary role in the customer decision-making process; and are always tied to specific needs. To compete effectively given ongoing, continuing market changes, customers have to be able to cope flexibly with the speed of change. To do this, customers want suppliers to offer flexible solutions to satisfy their needs. Customers also are facing an increasing pace of innovation and significantly shorter product life cycles. They need suppliers to help them to get to market quickly, achieve wide penetration quickly, and amortize costs. Your potential customers also face emerging and collapsing routes to market, and in response they need your support and creativity to simultaneously launch new products and trial new routes to market. To compete, your customers need an integrated and customized supply chain, and as a consequence want from you help achieving the goals of the supply chain *as a whole*, as well as its customization.

Perhaps the most important consideration is the understanding that your customers are driven by a combination of both cost and risk reduction. These can emerge from multiple points of origin. Cost savings may be derived from better information and reduced uncertainty. Accurate demand forecasting can help reduce costs as a result of resource optimization and market discounting. Elimination of duplicate or redundant processes can also reduce costs. This might require a systems-wide reconfiguration of processes to ensure that buyers do not expend resources on tasks you've already completed (e.g., quality and quantity checks, different processes across departments). Or diminished costs that might emerge from a better flow of supplies. This can be achieved through a tailoring of transaction procedures according to buyers' specifications and the elimination of superfluous handling.

Your knowledge and awareness can help customers achieve reduced costs by improving the efficiency of the supply chain, helping them identify overspecified products, unnecessary redundancies, or inefficient usage, which reduces the consumption of system inputs.

Application of a tighter quality control process also can help to control costs, which can be passed along to customers. You can help buyers to focus on the quality of their own processes by increasing the stringency of your own company's quality controls, leading to systemic improvement and resource conservation. This systemic improvement can lead to a minimization of wasted materials as rejected product and wasted service time are reduced. It also helps to minimize costs associated with handling, and remedying complaints derived from poor service or defective products. Effective steps taken in pursuit of a reduction in costs is a key signal customers understand.

Reduction of risk—like costs—is an enormous issue for potential customers. It is important, here, to research and understand the kinds of risks that your customer faces. They may face risks that are external to their relationships with suppliers, originating in the marketplace or their broader operating environment. These might include foreign substitute products, governmental regulations, and so on. They might also face risks that are internal to their relationships with suppliers, and that originate from these relationships, such as information security. To be successful, you have to get "inside the skin" of your customers in order to piece together their concerns. You have to become a detective, reading between the lines, to develop insights that are unlikely to be shared with you in an entirely transparent way—particularly as these pertain to functional vulnerabilities.

How do you reduce external and internal risks? With regard to external, market-based risks, sharing information on the market can help to reduce general transactional risk by facilitating transactional transparency. Asset-sharing plans can help to reduce the risks associated with a general down turn in demand, while supply chain integration can diminish risks associated with pricing pressures. In some ways, externally derived risks have a more straightforward control mechanism than internally derived risks, which tend to be somewhat more complex because they are idiosyncratic to the specific relationship. For example, trust that the supplier will pass on lower costs to the buyer diminishes opportunism on the part of partners and lowers risk of unexpected price increases—because the development of trust is the key level. From our discussion of relationship types, partner interdependence also diminishes risks associated with opportunism, such as withdrawal from the relationship. A future orientation—consistent with higher-level relationships—that encompasses joint planning can reduce risks associated with commitment to an inappropriately conceived or deployed strategy.

Action Steps for Developing In-Depth Customer Understanding:

- Identify customer needs
- Focus on reduction in risk
- Understand the customer's buying process
- Foster communication and encourage proactivity

Approaching communication and risk reduction effectively is a key signal of your commitment to customers.

Step 3: Customer Goal Setting (Determining Your Customer's Objectives)

Third, it is essential to develop a *topography* of customers' objectives. This is a process that is analytical, in that it depends on building a hierarchical analysis of the objectives of each account being targeted. The goal here is to develop an understanding of what advantages and disadvantages characterize each key account. Engaging this analytic approach will help the supplier understand the ways in which its products and/or services will enable potential clients to exploit these advantages, and to minimize disadvantages. This process also helps in the generation of powerful conclusions about key accounts' competitive situation. How do you go about doing this? Use any and all publically available information, annual reports, internal reports, newsletters, or secondary data sources that you are able to gather about the client to compile the most comprehensive view possible.

Action Steps for Determining Your Customer's Objectives:

- Research publicly available information
- Review past purchase history and behavior
- Understand customer's organization's strategic plan

Gaining insight in this fashion will help you determine how your organization might be of assistance to the client in the pursuit of their strategic goals.

Step 4: Present the Value That Matters
(Aligning Solutions with Customer Needs)

The summary that you generate from your analysis of this information should be synthesized in conjunction with the information you gather from the customer's objectives analysis. Through this synthesis, you can determine what impact your products and/or services can potentially have on the customer's bottom-line outcomes.

An analysis of a customer's internal value chain can help potential suppliers to understand how a key account actually functions. You can explore what problems and issues the customer faces through this analysis, with a focus on developing a plan to help resolve these issues through improvements and innovation. The effective utilization and integration of data reflecting the customer's own internal value chain can be a source for differentiation in the value chain—a point of leverage that you can exploit. But, it is also important that this is an intensive, iterative process that requires a disciplined focus, time, and patience. The critical patterns will not be immediately obvious to the casual—or even the interested—observer, and require a determined investigative analytic eye. However, the reward of adopting the focused, data-driven approach is that it is likely to make you a more strategic supplier in the eyes of customers—making the list.

> **Action Steps for Aligning Solutions with Customer Needs:**
> - Understand customer's supply chain
> - Identify and clarify how your solution impacts their business processes
> - Demonstrate the real value of your offering in their terms and language

There is not simply one avenue to becoming a strategic supplier. Rather, it is important to think about the wide range of ways in which to elevate your position with customers. There are numerous points of potential insertion that can facilitate entry into this new identity.

From the standpoint of inbound logistics, for example, you can introduce handling processes that minimize damage and lead to systematic marginal benefits. From an operations perspective, you can introduce unique product features, conform to established product specifications, provide a low defect rate, and be responsive to design changes. Outbound logistics also offers a point of leverage, through rapid and timely delivery, accurate order processing, and careful handling to reduce damage. Marketing and sales can be leveraged as well, through high sales force coverage, superior technical literature, advantageous credit terms, and personal relationships with buyers. Finally, through service your strategic positioning can be generated via rapid installation, high service quality, and wide service coverage. Of course, these are examples and represent only a small fraction of the potential mechanical drivers across the value chain that can be applied in this context.

Call to Action: Being an Active, Engaged Account Manager

In this chapter we set forth the case for account management. Organizations must use this valuable integrated, boundary-spanning function to better identify and synchronize with customer needs. The value that an active, engaged account manager can uncover can be the key to ensuring sustainable competitive advantage in the marketplace as the sales function is best utilized, directed, and driven toward meeting customer needs, not just today, but in the future as well. As authors, we challenge you to review your customer base and determine the value of segmenting your customers. Our next chapters focus on how to implement this segmentation, but it is first necessary to understand the usefulness of the approach and how it can impact your competitive position.

Endnotes

1   Grosfeld-Nir, A., Ronen, B., & Kozlovsky, N. (2007). The Pareto managerial principle: when does it apply?. *International Journal of Production Research*, *45*(10), 2317–2325.

Chapter 5

Building the Account Portfolio

"Awareness requires a rupture with the world we take for granted;
then old categories of experience are called into question and
revised."

—Shoshana Zuboff

M arielle, an account manager at Perry Products, was struggling to decide what to do about the possible expansion of their business with Mitchell Belle Salons. PP was making money there—good money. They weren't devoting a lot of time or effort to maintaining the relationship—in some ways the relationship was on auto pilot. But, the customer was looking to expand their business with PP to a broader range of both products and services. This was going to require a substantial capital investment in both manufacturing and distribution infrastructure. But, she just wasn't sure that this was the right decision—what was wrong? They were making money, so why was she hesitant to target resources there? Although this was more of a gut feeling, or maybe even a sixth-sense kind of response, it didn't feel like the Mitchell business really fit with PP's core long-term strategic focus. In some ways the Mitchell business was actually a stretch for PP, even though it was profitable. She needed some way to methodically evaluate Mitchell relative to PP's other businesses—but how?

THE PURPOSE OF THIS CHAPTER is to frame a process for thinking systematically about how to understand the potential current and future value attributable to extant accounts. This categorization facilitates the development of a coherent resource allocation strategy with the goal of maximizing account value. In this chapter, we'll focus on explicit differentiation of accounts based on their attractiveness and supplier's strength with the account. These descriptive "fields" serve as the foundation for the emergence of four distinct account categories—Strategic accounts, Star accounts, Status accounts, and Streamline accounts.[1] Placement of accounts into these categories helps to define each account's current value to the supplier. Through this categorization process we describe an approach to channel organization resources to these accounts, coinciding with these categorizations, and value that can be maximized. This analytic process requires a deep reciprocal knowledge of customers relative to suppliers' own strategic focus and competitive position with the account. Our goal is to provide insight into the process of account analysis and resource allocation based on the systematic categorization of accounts within a portfolio matrix.[2]

When trying to determine the importance and necessity of categorizing and selecting which accounts to sell and service, and to what extent resources should be allocated to those accounts, we need not look beyond the statistics and metrics associated with customer relationship management and lifetime value. Based on decades of research, it is evident that accounts can be separated into different categories and these categories are representative of different levels of profit. In many circumstances, the Pareto principle holds true: 80 percent of your profits come from 20 percent of your accounts. Rising customer acquisition costs and increased competition emphasize the importance of retaining valuable customers, and perhaps letting go of those that aren't as valuable. This allows us to put more emphasis on growth for larger potential accounts. To this end, research shows that a new prospect or weak current account can have profit margins that, on average, are up to 20 percent but in some circumstances may actually cost you money! Alternatively, selling to a current, high potential account may yield profits as high as 60 percent.

Beyond profitability as a metric, there is also the idea of word of mouth. Whether you are selling in a business-to-business or business-to-consumer world, sales veterans can tell you, "It is a small world out there." A bad customer service experience or selling interaction reaches up to 10 people while the best service often goes unpublicized. Typically, for every customer that bothers to complain, 26 others will remain silent! And, more importantly, for every complaint that exists, it takes an average of 12 positive interactions to compensate and overcome that one negative past experience. Last year alone, over 80 percent of customers stopped doing business with a supplier or salesperson because of a bad customer experience. Needless to say, the importance of identifying high value and high potential customers cannot be understated.

Developing an analytical framework for understanding relative account value, the objective for this chapter, presents a systematic way of conducting account analysis and placement within a portfolio matrix structure. We describe an approach to the evaluation of accounts that creates greater transparency regarding their ultimate financial and strategic value to suppliers, with direct implications for the optimization of tactical resource allocations in the service of these accounts. We will begin by describing the two functional axes along which all accounts vary—attractiveness and strength—and how to define and describe both. We will detail how simultaneous variation along these axes defines the placement of key accounts within a two-by-two portfolio matrix structure. We then will develop the link between account placement and tactical resource allocation. Finally, we offer technical insight into how this account analysis and placement emerges, and discuss resource allocation implications following account analysis and the implementation of the portfolio approach.

What Is the Portfolio Structure?

The portfolio structure is a conceptual framework for planning. It serves as a mechanism to guide the behaviors of account managers seeking to deploy organizational resources in the most effective way. This is done in an effort to maximize CLV (customer lifetime value). It also is a framework that is easily transferrable to a range of key areas, including product management, territory management, division management and subsidiary management as well. The portfolio structure—similar to the BCG matrix in the strategic management domain—is used to segregate accounts into distinct categories, with consequent implications for the functional configuration of sales plans and the tactical deployment of resources.

Adoption of the portfolio structure for account management planning purposes requires that accounts be systematically distinguished from one another using criteria that ultimately impact the potential generation of customer lifetime value. Accounts can be classified as falling along two continua—attractiveness and strength. Attractiveness reflects the ability of an account to deliver value to a supplier. On the other side of the coin, supplier strength reflects the ability of the supplier to deliver value to the account. Accounts can be distinguished in this way by focusing on the interaction between their attractiveness to the supplier, and the supplier's strength with the account. These values range from high to low levels of attractiveness, and high to low levels of supplier strength. Customer attractiveness encompasses the alignment of the account with the organization's broader strategic goals, the account's *projected* lifetime value—how much business is forecasted—and the transactional risk associated with the account. In contrast, supplier strength with the account encompasses the current level of actual business with the account, the supplier's competitive standing in relation to all other potential suppliers in the market, and relationships and structures in place within the account.

Figure 5.1. The Decision Matrix

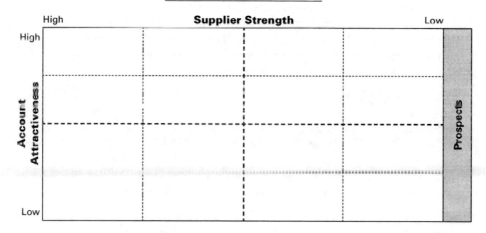

What can be determined from this bimodal referencing process is that the portfolio structure results in a two-by-two matrix. Within this matrix emerge four distinct account categories. While these categories are conceptually mutually exclusive, they are not *necessarily* functionally exclusive. Given the inherent dynamism in the customer relationship management process, these categories potentially retain some overlap and should be looked at as being a snapshot of the *current* status quo, and continuously in flux. Their inherent dynamism within the portfolio highlights the need to regularly audit the classification of accounts into distinct categories.[3] Here, it is important to note that the matrix applies to the categorization of current accounts—prospects remain undetermined with regard either to their attractiveness or to relative supplier strength. Prospects occupy a role in the matrix, but maintain only an auxiliary position in the planning and resource allocation process. Although the ultimate goal for all prospects is the generation of revenue, the centrality of their positioning in the resource allocation process is "currently" undetermined. Across the cells or categories within the matrix, as noted above, accounts can be rated high or low across two criteria—attractiveness and strength—and as a consequence fall into four customer categories: Strategic, Star, Status, and Streamline. "Strategic" customers fall into the high-attractiveness/high-strength category, "Star" customers fall into the high-attractiveness/low-strength category, "Status" customers fall into the low-attractiveness/high-strength category, while "Streamline" customers fall into the low-attractiveness/low-strength category, as detailed in Figure 5.2.

Maximizing Value across Customer Categories

The significant consequence associated with adoption of the portfolio structure is to distinguish customers from one another, and to categorize them systematically into groups. As we've sought to establish in earlier chapters of this book, the ultimate goal for all customers is to maximize "value." What value means depends on the source from which value is derived—in this case from which customer categories. Different customers ultimately require different tactical approaches to help them generate value. Let's consider this example:

> A football coach can field only 11 players at a time. Throughout the game the coach makes decisions about which players to bring in, depending on the circumstances on the field. The "jumbo package," with a strong blocking fullback, is great in short yardage situations to avoid turning the ball over on downs. The jumbo package also can help a team cross the goal line to score from the opponent's one-yard line. This package generates value in circumstances when the ball only has to be moved a short distance, options are limited by the available depth of the field, and the eyes of the defense can be focused toward fewer, more tractable hotspots.

> The same package is less likely to generate value if the ball is first and 10 on the opposition's 40-yard line. There's no reason to move the ball one or two yards when the field is wide open and all of the north-south variables are in play. However, a fast receiver with good hands and great height is less likely to generate value when the ball is first and goal. The wideout generates value under different circumstances than the blocking fullback—but both are strategic to the overall game plan, and their attributes have to be understood for that value to emerge.

Understanding where customer value comes from, and how to maximize customer value, only comes with a systematic understanding of your portfolio of customers. Different customers— or more accurately—customers in different portfolio categories—require different approaches to maximize returns on the investment of scarce organizational resources.

Customers in different categories vary in the extent to which they utilize suppliers' products or services, the nature of the relationship they share, and the competitive status of suppliers. With regard to functional contact, the strategic approach adopted toward customers, the managerial competencies needed to maximize value, the nature of the resources allocated, and product deployment also differ. The tactical approach to price and promotion, product distribution profile, communication patterns, and communication content also vary across customer categories. Finally, just as a coach maintains distinct goals for each player deployed during a game, the goals in place for customers in different categories also should be distinct. All of these variables play a role in the categorization of accounts.

Star Customers

Star customers, falling in the high-attractiveness/low-strength category, align with the supplier's strategic focus, have a fairly high projective CLV, and represent a relatively low level of risk. However, these customers also currently underutilize available products and services and retain only a basic or cooperative relationship with the supplier. The competitive status of the supplier is neutral-to-disadvantaged, and in order to maximize value suppliers should adopt an opportunistic approach toward the customer—seeking to build business and increase points of leverage. The key managerial competency most essential to the negotiation of Star customers is a developed entrepreneurial orientation, with an emphasis on the selective or tactical investment of resources to enhance market differentiation and facilitate an expansion of current offerings. It also is crucial to preserve an aggressive pricing focus with Star customers, to price and promote for an increased share of their business—moving them toward Strategic customer status. With regard to distribution, and given limited relational strength with Star customers, controlled expansion is most likely. Communication with Stars also should be maintained through an account team via institutional channels, with just enough information being shared to overcome expansion barriers. The strategic goal with Star customers is to increase revenues as you incrementally change the nature of their business focus.

Strategic Customers

Strategic customers share some similarities with Stars, but have some clear points of distinction as well. Strategic customers align well with suppliers, representing deep long-term business opportunity. They don't pose obvious transactional risks. Because of their high relative strength, products and services tend to see an increasing utilization, creating a relationship status that is either interdependent or integrated, and a competitive status that is advantaged. The strategic approach to adopt vis-à-vis Strategic customers is to enhance value by building and expanding. The managerial competency most likely to generate value is as a business developer—to expand current product and service offerings and consumption. Resource investment should be heavy, in recognition of their high potential CLV. With customers in this category, the focus should be on maximizing the expansion of products/services lines, with an emphasis on price leadership, and passing on economics of scale to these quasi-partners to help tighten relational ties. Suppliers' targets should include a broadening of distribution to maximize revenues, and communications with Strategic customers that are transparent and heavy at the team, institutional, department, and executive levels to ensure full transparency and relationship maintenance. The ultimate goal for Strategic customers is to increase revenues and profits.

Status Customers

Status customers, who are low on attractiveness and high on strength, share some similarities with Star and Strategic customers, but also some points of distinction as well. Status customers tend not to align strategically with suppliers' goals, may have a relatively low potential customer lifetime value, and may also present some transactional risks. So why are these attractive? Suppliers' products and services are fully utilized by Status customers, they share a cooperative if not integral relationship, and their competitive status is advantaged-to-neutral. Because of low overlap with strategic goals, lower levels of potential value, and the riskiness of the involvement, suppliers are well served to either maintain or to reverse course in their strategic approach with Status customers in order to refocus on profit maximization. The competency most likely to generate maximum value from Status customers is the managerial competency, while resource allocations made in the service of these accounts should be maintained, or the progressive imposition of limits instituted. In regard to product orientation, suppliers should prune unprofitable items, and prices should be stabilized. Wide distribution levels should be maintained with Status customers, but only until a more sustainable long-term approach can be established. Communication with customers in this category should be conducted across multiple levels (at the account team, the institutional level, and the department level)—given their inherent long-term strategic incompatibility and low growth potential, information sharing should be constrained. The goal for Status customers should be the maximization of profits.

Streamline Customers

In the fourth cell of the portfolio matrix are Streamline customers. These customers have low projected lifetime value, their business doesn't tend to coincide with suppliers' long-term strategic goals, and their engagement represents a nontrivial level of operational risk. Streamline customers don't generate a great deal of current revenue, due to a declining level of utilization of suppliers' products and services. These customers frequently do business with other suppliers and thus suppliers have only a neutral-to-disadvantaged relationship with them—and the relationship they share is basic. The strategic approach toward maximization of value from these customers is to manage for cash and continually assess the future of the relationship. Tacticians—or tactically skilled managers—are best positioned to squeeze value from Streamline customers, systematically refocusing resources toward other accounts. Aggressive pruning of unprofitable products, raising prices, and minimizing promotions also increases potential value. Suppliers should gradually withdraw from unprofitable areas, communication with Streamline customers should be institutional, information sharing should be extremely limited and controlled, and the goal for these customers should be the maintenance of profits.

Figure 5.2. Categorizing the Portfolio

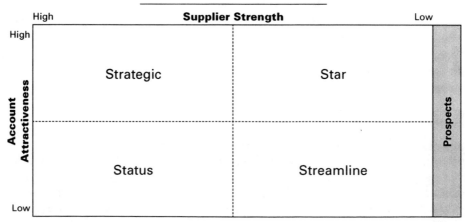

Portfolio Generation

Establishing a portfolio—or the development of a process for evaluating the parameters of all current business—depends on the systematic analysis of all current accounts. Planning, selling, and the coherent management of business activities can only be efficiently and effectively driven if all of the preliminary data collection and investigation associated with these processes is both accurate and relevant to the task(s) at hand. The primary goal of the account analysis process is the alignment of current accounts into one of four categories that most directly reflect their potential lifetime value; influencing the nature of the resource allocations deployed in the service of these accounts.

It is necessary here to reiterate that resource allocation is by its very nature a lagged process—decisions are made about the future deployment of resources, which involves an estimation or an assessment of future (unknowable) conditions. Thus, the process of account analysis is inherently predictive, in that it functions in a probabilistic way through forecasting, where regression based historical patterns are used to make guesses as to the future of an account and its relationship with a supplier. As noted above, accounts exist in a space that is constantly in flux. It is less about an account's current position—which is "known" in an objective way—than it is about its anticipated immediate or intermediate future position. The latter is what defines the category (or often categories) into which an account falls (or is expected to fall) within the portfolio matrix.

The accurate classification of an account into a particular category depends on a deep, faithful, and relevant understanding not only of the customer, but also of the nature of the relationship between the customer and supplier, core infrastructure, and key relational variables. In order to generate an analysis that ultimately and successfully encapsulates the essentially subjective future value attributable to the account, it is crucial to draw data and other information from several sources that reflect on this value. Although the value is subjective, because it depends on judgments based on a dynamic set of interactions, it can also be extremely accurate (ultimately) if the range of input driving the value is wide and appropriate. Key sources of account analysis include internal financial data, internal account databases, sales representatives or primary contacts, the account team or secondary contacts, direct customer contact, and other syndicated research.

It may at first blush be surprising that the first two elements necessary for generating account analysis are sources that are internal to the supplier. But, in light of the foundationally relational drivers of account value in this status, it is strategic to start with an inward focus before actually analyzing accounts. This inward focus on self-knowledge is by no means a novel or new concept—"Know Thyself," an ancient Greek aphorism, is a Delphic maxim that was by tradition given by the Oracle of Delphi and was inscribed in the forecourt of the Temple of Apollo. The entire field of strategic management and a multibillion-dollar annual business in strategic consultation depends on a foundational internal (and external) analysis.

SWOT Analysis

The *SWOT analysis* (**S**trengths, **W**eaknesses, **O**pportunities, and **T**hreats) is a broadly applied analytical tool that provides a systematic planning architecture for the evaluation of the (internal) strengths and weakness and (external) opportunities and threats associated with an account, business, product, project, or industry. Albert Humphrey, a business consultant with expertise in organizational change, is recognized as having developed the SWOT analysis process at Stanford University as a strategic planning method in the 1960s and '70s. Central to SWOT analysis are the explicit or stated goals and objectives associated with a particular account, business, or project. These goals and objectives serve as an explicit point of departure for conducting the analysis, and essentially define the upper and lower-level boundaries of the SWOT variables. Strategic fit reflects the extent that a supplier is able to match its resource deployments to the available market opportunities, given its goals and objectives for those opportunities. Profitability ultimately emerges through the effective utilization of the supplier's resources. This begins with an understanding of what those resources are and how they can contribute to the value of any given customer.

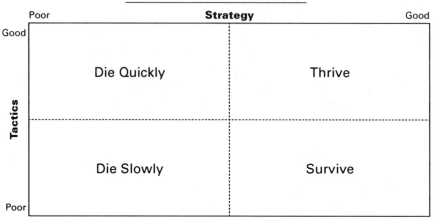

Figure 5.3. Account Planning SWOT

Strengths, an internal supplier characteristic, are reflective of the attributes of a supplier's business that lend advantage over competitors in the marketplace seeking the same business, contributing to more effective negotiation of market obstacles. Strengths are those things that a supplier does well and lead to differentiation from the competition, and potentially include factors such as systematic production efficiencies, well-developed distribution networks, capital, strong products, processes, and structures. Weaknesses, in contrast, also an internal supplier characteristic, reflect the attributes of the same supplier that lead to a disadvantage relative to other competitors, where improvement is needed and skills or capacities are lacking.

Examples of weakness potentially include low market saturation, newness, high operating costs, weak products, processes, and structures. Opportunities, an attribute of the external market environment in which the supplier operates, reflect vulnerabilities of which a supplier can take advantage. Opportunities include dissolution of competitors' contracts, changing market demographics, and technological innovation. Threats, also an external market attribute, represent any factors that might diminish a supplier's competitive position, including governmental regulation, lawsuits, and low-cost foreign-market entrants.

The SWOT analysis allows for a better determination toward which specific account resource deployments are most likely to result in substantial marginal incremental returns. Such resource deployments are directly impacted by where in the portfolio matrix each account falls—again always with an eye toward profit and CLV maximization. As noted above, the position of accounts in the matrix is determined by account attractiveness and supplier strength. Attractiveness depends on the account's ability to deliver value to your organization. Whether attractiveness is high or low depends on the strategic alignment of the account with the organization's broader goals, the projected lifetime value of the account and transactional risks associated with the business. Supplier strength reflects the organization's ability to deliver value to the account. Whether strength is high or low is influenced by the degree of current business with the account, relative competitive standing, relationships, and structures in place. Placement of accounts into the four quadrants of the portfolio matrix depends on the answers to these 18 diagnostic questions.

The 18-Question Diagnostic

In order to deploy resources in the service of accounts in the most impactful way possible (i.e., to generate the most value), it is essential that they be positioned within the matrix appropriately. Placement is contingent on understanding both the attractiveness of the account and the supplier's strength with the account, which interact to determine where the account falls in the portfolio matrix.

Account Attractiveness

As we've noted above, attractiveness depends on strategic alignment, projected lifetime value, and the risk associated with an account. The first nine diagnostic questions, the answers to which must be classified as being either "High" or "Low," can be used to help establish how attractive an account is. In order to create a score for an account, do the following:

- Responses to each question should be given either a "+" or a "–".

- Tally of the " I s" should be made for categorization as being high or low on account attractiveness.

- Remember that these evaluations provide an answer to only half of the equation necessary for account analysis and portfolio matrix categorization. The second half of the equation centers on the question of the strength of the account.

Strategic alignment. The first three questions are used to evaluate strategic alignment:

1. What types of products/services does the customer need?

If these products/services coincide with suppliers' primary manufacturing area, then this is suggestive of strategic alignment ("high"). If customers' products/services needs fall along a more auxiliary or peripheral competency spectrum, then there is less strategic alignment ("low").

2. Where/how is the customer accessing these products/services?

If access is to products and services generated largely through primary channels of distribution, then this is reflective of strategic alignment, as it allows the supplier to leverage available efficiencies. In contrast, if products/services are indirectly accessed through third-party avenues or subsidiary channels, there is less strategic alignment with the customer, as the costs of distribution are likely to be much higher.

3. How does the customer use these products/services?

If the customer needs are met though the standard, full-spectrum of off-the-shelf products and services, then strategic alignment is high as the margins in standard products are better. In contrast, if the customer uses only a subset of products/services and/or those that are used require customization or special preparation, the alignment is likely to be lower as costs to the supplier rise in response to "particular" customer needs.

Projected lifetime value (PLV). These three questions can be used to evaluate lifetime value:

4. What are the opportunities for entry/expansion?

If the account has a growing business with a wide range of needs and underdeveloped supplier relationships, then the opportunities are higher and PLV is also higher. If the account is operating a mature business with established supply chain relationships, then these opportunities are likely to be lower and PLV also as a consequence is lower.

5. What are the barriers to entry/expansion?

If the account is operating in a highly regulated industry for example, or consumes high tech products and services, this can inhibit the emergence of competitors and increase PLV as competition is likely to be lower. If in contrast there are fewer legislative constraints or technological hurdles, projected lifetime value is likely to be less as competitors can more easily emerge.

6. Are there any extraordinary limitations to customer lifetime value?

If the customer is operating with soft money, for example, or is operating on a contract basis, then customer lifetime value is likely to be lower as the horizon of the business relationship is necessarily explicitly definable. Absent these points of functional terminus, where the customer's business doesn't have any imposed business constraints, CLV is likely to be higher.

Account risk. Earlier, in Chapter 4, we highlighted the importance of understanding the customer's business, the customer's strategic contingencies, and the range of factors at play in their operating environment. Evaluation of account risk, through the final three Attractiveness questions, highlights the importance of understanding the customer's business. Thus, to determine account risk, it is necessary first to establish:

7. What is the customer's current business climate?

If the customer's operating environment is at a point of relative equilibrium, where business relationships are "fairly" static and their business is essentially "predictable"—to the point where that is possible—these climate factors are likely to diminish account risk. In contrast, if the customer is exposed to legal issues, their core technology is in a period of flux, or offshore competition is emerging, then the risk associated with the customer is higher.

8. What is the customer's competitive standing in its industry?

Again, it is clear that understanding the customer's business is essential both for adding value, but also for assessing customers' potential value. If the customer is a leader in their industry, and their visibility is fairly well entrenched, the transactional risk associated with their business is likely to be lower. In contrast, if the customer is essentially camouflaged by their competition, there is likely to be greater uncertainty involved with their business.

9. What intangible factors are affecting attractiveness?

Personal relationships, personality, and congruence of values all potentially serve as intangibles that affect attractiveness. When personal relationships are good, when personalities "click" and when the values of the supplier coincide with those of the customer, the intangibles are high, and the relationship is likely to be maintained with greater equilibrium and fewer bumps in the road. In contrast, when relationships are difficult to navigate, when personalities clash, and there is low value congruence, the intangibles also are lower, diminishing the smoothness of key boundary-spanning relationships.

Final tally for Attractiveness questions (total number of +s):

Strength of the Account

In order to fully analyze accounts within the portfolio matrix, it is also necessary to quantify account strength. Strength with the account is reflected by three related variables—current business, competitive standing, and relationships and structures. Again, nine diagnostic questions can be asked to help to classify the strength of the supplier with an account on a continuum ranging from high to low.

In order to score each account using the next nine diagnostic "strength" questions, do the following:

- Understand that the number serves a diagnostic purpose of categorizing accounts based on their strength. Each question should be given either a "+" or a "−."•   Tally of the "+s" should be made for categorization as being high or low on Account Strength.

- The score from the Account Attractiveness calculation should then be matched with the current score, and the account placed within the matrix accordingly.

Current Business. Current business strength can be determined by a set of questions that have a straightforward financial interpretation:

10. What is the current level of customer product/service utilization?

If utilization of products is high (relative to established customer-specific criteria) then utilization is high. If, in contrast, utilization is low, again in consideration of customer-specific usage metrics, then utilization levels are low. Defining "low" and "high" in this status is necessarily a subjective evaluation. Evaluating utilization levels depends on a specified, articulated set of customer expectations.

11. What are the current service levels?

If accounts utilize products which are systematically decoupled from ancillary revenue-generating service offerings, then the answer to this question would be "low." In contrast, if products and services are consistently effectively bundled, and products/services offerings are purchased in tandem, then the answer to this question would be "high."

12. What are the current growth trends across all products and services?

If quarter after quarter the revenue associated with an account continues to increase, and the range of products and services consumed continues to widen, then growth trends are positive. In contrast, if there is a contraction in the range of product/service offerings the account purchases, then the growth trend is low.

Competitive standing. In addition to current business levels, it also is essential to understand where your organization stands relative to firms competing for the same business. The diagnostic questions used to assess competitive viability are:

13. How do we rate vs. current competitive suppliers?

If pricing is lower, quality is higher, and distribution more reliable than other current providers, then competitive standing is likely to be high. In contrast, if pricing, quality, and distribution issues are not definitive, then competitive standing relative to the current competition is lower. Although current competition is likely most acutely in focus, it also is important to account for future potential competition.

14. How do we compare to prospective competitive suppliers?

This question highlights consideration of the horizon, with its emergent technologies and capabilities. If other suppliers are able to leverage available channels of distribution or supply chain innovations your company has not yet adopted, then competitive standing relative to prospective competition is likely to be low. In contrast, if your organization is leveraging the most contemporary tools and innovation in its business, then prospective competition is less likely to be at a competitive advantage.

15. How difficult would it be to close competitive gaps?

If gaps have emerged as a consequence of neglect of infrastructure, or issues of capacity, these are likely to be relatively straightforward to deal with; and the answer to this question would be fairly low. In contrast, if gaps have emerged as a consequence of a failure to innovate, invest or support sufficient human capital to maintain state-of-the-art processes and structures, these gaps are more difficult to close.

Relationships and structures. Supplier strength also is affected by the nature of the relationships between key boundary spanners, and the structures in place for the movement of material and products/services. The answers to the following questions are reflective of this aspect of supplier strength.

16. How strong are the current point-of-contact relationships?

These relationships have clear potential to significantly affect the nature of ongoing as well as potential future business with customers. If these relationships are effective, and the principals involved have a clear line of sight with one another, then the answer to this question is "high." If there are differences of personality among boundary spanners on either end of the supplier-customer relationship, then this can create turbulence that diminishes the strength of these relationships.

17. How developed are the departmental and executive relationships?

Beyond the operational interactions of the boundary spanners in tactical or functional positions are those at the departmental or executive level. Again, if these relationships are congenial and regularly reinforced, then the answer here is high. If these relationships are infrequently maintained or if they are they're characterized by disagreements and unpleasantness, then the answer to this question is "low."

18. How strong are our capabilities for supply and distribution?

Outside of the personalities of the boundary spanners across organizational levels are the strategic infrastructural elements that make supply possible. If supply and distribution capabilities are sufficient to accommodate the business, then the answer here is likely to be high. In light of inherent turbulence and market changes, the answer here is also contingent on the shifting landscape defining relationships with customers. If customers' needs are consistently being left unmet, then the answer to this question is "low."

Final tally for Strength questions (total number of +s): [   ]

Categorization

Once accounts have been analyzed through this diagnostic process, it is essential then to use the insight developed through this process to actively categorize them and deploy resources accordingly. As we noted in Chapter 4, the core or essential aspect of the account management role is the focused resource allocation to accounts with the goal of maximizing the value of the account to the supplier. Categorization enables you to capture a snapshot of your accounts' current positions, project future changes in these positions, and develop plans as to the most appropriate resource allocation strategy for the account. This process requires a disciplined reliance upon and application of data. Trusting your own ability to make decisions as to how to think about accounts isn't easy, particularly for young or inexperienced business people. To facilitate these judgments, the use of tested tools like the portfolio matrix can help generate more confidence in your decisions. Putting account analysis to work means making decisions based on a systematic evaluation of a range of specific criteria, and placing accounts within your portfolio based on these analyses. Inherent to account analysis is the positioning of accounts which bleeds over into the categorization process, which also inherently encompasses prediction of future account position.

For example, accounts in the Strategic customer category are *lynchpin accounts*—this means that they are both lucrative and directly coincide with suppliers' strategic aims. These accounts should be grown. However, if these accounts are smaller accounts, analysis provides a tactical or functional map that can be used to determine where resources should be deployed in the service of these accounts with the specific goal of increasing their size. For example, if the customer uses only a narrow spectrum of available products/services offerings, changes in the value of the account may be accessible through investments designed to help customers understand how a broader range of products/services could facilitate their business goals. This point of leverage, again, highlights the importance of developing and maintaining a deep, current understanding of all aspects of key customers' business. Doing so provides insights into the various ways in which a full(er) spectrum of supplier's products and services can help the customer more effectively attain their own strategic goals. Insight, that resources should be invested to enhance customers' awareness of the functional benefits of additional products and services, emerges directly through account analysis.

Accounts in the Status category, however, represent an entirely different frame of value than strategic accounts. The business represented by these customers is lucrative and generates value, but it doesn't coincide strategically with the long-term business objectives of the supplier. Resources invested in the service of these customers, therefore, do not—from the standpoint of infrastructure—directly facilitate long-term strategic goals. They might be worthwhile and important because they generate value, but they are viewed as strategically nonessential or replaceable. Thus, resource deployments in the service of these Status customers should be maintained, if possible, to retain the revenue stream they represent. However, whether these customers are currently small or large, resources targeted toward them should not be increased or modified substantially, in light of their long-term incongruence with the supplier's ultimate strategic goals.

Star customers represent a different resource allocation challenge. In this case, the business generated by these customers is strategically congruent with suppliers' long-term goals. Because these customers represent a lucrative, strategically coherent business with an as-yet unfulfilled value potential, resources should be deployed tactically to *edge* them toward the Strategic category. Insight into how to deploy resources in the most effective way *vis-à-vis* Star customers emerges through account analysis. For example, if strength with the customer is low because current capabilities for supply or distribution are underdeveloped, resources should be allocated toward infrastructural improvements to increase these capabilities. These kinds of structural investments aimed to increase strength with the account are justifiable—the account is serviced because, unlike with Status customers, the business is strategically congruent. The ultimate value associated with these investments will continue to grow as a consequence.

Finally, although Streamline customers also represent a lucrative current source of revenue, in the short term, they are both a strategically incongruent business, and also underutilize available product/service offerings. Through account analysis, it can be established that their value ultimately is not sustainable in the long term. As a consequence of the functional and structural mismatch Streamline customers represent, suppliers should *squeeze* as much value as can be derived from the business as possible in the short term. Rather than actively increasing—or even sustaining—current levels, resources should be drawn away from these customers as expeditiously as possible. However, the resource withdrawal should be executed tactically, with an explicit focus on camouflage, so as to prevent any kind of otherwise avoidable catastrophic loss of revenue. Although Streamline customers are strategically expendable, there is no functional benefit associated with precipitating a premature loss of the revenue stream their business represents.

Steps for Success: Account Categorization

Throughout the book, we've focused on the most appropriate allocation of account-focused resources. Here we will offer practical guidance in the form of quick/summary action steps for making critical resource allocation decisions correctly. This requires that accounts be categorized in the most transparent way from the perspective of achieving maximum CLV. Categorization serves as the foundation for correct resource allocation decisions. How would you put account analysis to work?

1   Steps involved in placement

Establishing customer attractiveness—requires answering these questions:

- What is the level of strategic alignment of the account (+/-)?
- What is the projected lifetime value of the account (+/-)?
- What is the level of risk associated with the account (+/-)?

Establishing supplier strength—requires answering these questions:

- What is the level of current business with the account (+/-)?
- What is the supplier's competitive standing with the account (+/-)?
- What relationships and structures are currently in place (+/-)?

continues

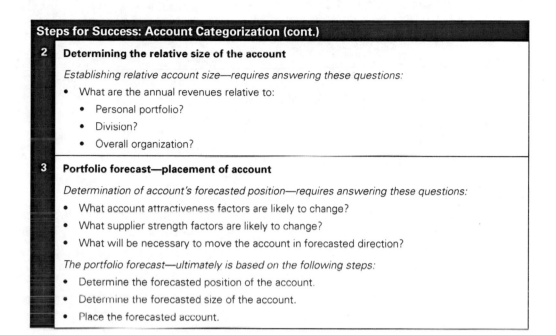

Steps for Success: Account Categorization (cont.)
2 **Determining the relative size of the account**
Establishing relative account size—requires answering these questions:
• What are the annual revenues relative to:
• Personal portfolio?
• Division?
• Overall organization?
3 **Portfolio forecast—placement of account**
Determination of account's forecasted position—requires answering these questions:
• What account attractiveness factors are likely to change?
• What supplier strength factors are likely to change?
• What will be necessary to move the account in forecasted direction?
The portfolio forecast—ultimately is based on the following steps:
• Determine the forecasted position of the account.
• Determine the forecasted size of the account.
• Place the forecasted account.

Call to Action: Steps for Resource Allocation

In closing, this chapter seeks to encourage firms to begin to view their accounts as a portfolio in order to make important strategic resource deployment decisions geared to profit and CLV maximization efforts. Toward that goal, the reader is encouraged to use the above tools to classify, categorize, and identify those accounts which warrant the most attention moving forward, those most strategically in synch with the objectives of the firm. If a customer is consuming more resources than it is worth, efforts should be taken to shift it from the portfolio. However, other firms will be identified as key strategic targets going forward. Use this chapter and its tools to regain competitive advantage in your market today.

Endnotes

1   Knox, S., Payne, A., Ryals, L., Maklan, S., & Peppard, J. (2012). *Customer relationship management.* Routledge.

2   *Ibid.*

3   Homburg, C., Workman Jr, J. P., & Jensen, O. (2002). A configurational perspective on key account management. *The Journal of Marketing*, 38–60.

tsv6

Chapter 6

Forecasting, KPIs, and Customer Portfolio Management

"[I]f customers constitute the most important asset a company possesses . . . then why not manage them like we manage the rest of the company assets?"

—Unknown

Brian, an account manager for the Rand Product Group, faced a dilemma as to whether to customize a peripheral line for Marshall Products, or risk losing the business to Stem Co., a market competitor. He could figure out the short-term costs of customizing the offering for Marshall. What was really getting in his head was that he didn't have the right data to determine whether RPG was even making money with Marshall. They'd been on the books for at least five years. But, there'd been so many nonstandard transactions that the Marshall bottom line was too fuzzy to read. Although he could manage the request, he just didn't know whether it made financial sense to do it. Brian just couldn't figure out what it would cost him to lose the business. He didn't want to lose a cash cow to Stem, but he also didn't want to continue to subsidize a money pit if he'd be better off without it. He needed some way to ground his decision in hard financials, but he had no idea what the right numbers to look at were or where he could find them.

THE PURPOSE OF THIS CHAPTER is to illustrate the importance of adopting a methodology that provides a disciplined focus on customers, understanding their underlying firm-specific value, and the metrics that ultimately are reflective of this value. This approach is essential for the establishment of customer relationship management practices that contribute to the implementation of strategic goals. In this chapter, we focus on factors that inhibit effective customer relationship management, discrete customer buying phases, and goals that emerge through this process. We also focus on the benefits and drawbacks associated with a range of key performance indicators (KPIs), criteria for their use in evaluation, and drivers of customer purchasing behavior. Understanding KPIs and purchasing catalysts facilitates the systematic maximization of outcomes from resources devoted toward customers and relationship management. We also devote attention to the development of customer portfolios, metrics for evaluation, and the tactical implications underlying the use of a customer portfolio management approach to value maximization. Our goal in this chapter is to increase the salience and insight into the relevance of criteria for the evaluation and disposition of customers and customer-focused resources.

How customers define themselves within the context of relationships with suppliers and what being a customer means has become increasingly complex and nuanced. As a consequence of these changing dynamics, the effective management of customers today has taken on aspects of both art and science that require a disciplined focus on data-driven processes. Today, almost one-third (32 percent) of customers are not profitable. In the face of increasingly tight competitive margins, the onus has shifted to suppliers to make sound customer-sourcing decisions. For example, revenues from the top 30 percent of customers based on lifetime value metrics are 33 percent higher than the top 30 percent of customers selected using less-value-focused metrics. Further, profits from the top 5 percent of customers based on assessments of lifetime value are 10–15 percent higher compared with the top 5 percent of customers using other metrics. Incredible as this may seem, in light of the ever-increasing expense associated with the generation and retention of customer value, 81 percent of companies today cannot quantify the actual dollar costs associated with a customer complaint! These companies do not know, have not measured, and have no system in place to evaluate the bottom-line impact of customer dissatisfaction on their business. Even more incredibly, 75 percent of companies today do not know the costs associated with the acquisition of a new customer. Although millions of dollars are spent each year sourcing customers, fully three-fourths of companies today cannot quantify these expenses on a per-customer basis. Finally, and perhaps most shocking, is that 50 percent of companies today do not know their organization's annual customer retention rates! This is true. Half of companies today do not track and cannot report annual churn. Given the extreme costs associated with sourcing, retention, and effective management, it is essential that attention and resources be devoted toward understanding the metrics that facilitate intelligent customer-focused decision-making.

The objectives for this chapter are to provide insight into the importance and value associated with critical, illustrative customer-based metrics and the development of decisions derived from these metrics. We describe the barriers to effective CRM, the three customer buying phases, and the issues most salient to customers during each phase. We detail several pivotal aspects of the goal-setting process, forecasting essentials, and approaches to forecasting. We also focus on traditional and customer-based marketing metrics, exploring the pros and cons associated with these various measures. We will examine issues related to market share, problems and pitfalls with the metric, and its relationship with both size-of-wallet and share-of-wallet metrics. Finally, we discuss strategic customer-based value metrics, highlighting past customer value, customer lifetime value, and customer equity, with an ultimate point of convergence being a systematic approach to customer portfolio management.

The New Customer

An underlying theme that we have tried to highlight throughout our writing in this book is that the nature of what we think of as a "customer" has changed in fundamental ways, and is continuing to change as the technologies and structures that support the market increasingly become more sophisticated and more democratic. Just as market transparencies have empowered customers, the tactics, approaches, and tools that enable suppliers to serve customers in a competitive fashion also have continued to change. Essentially, the arms race to successfully win and to keep customers has evolved in a symbiotic way evening the playing field on which suppliers compete for ever-more-elusive business. Historically customers were essentially at the mercy of an opaque system. Today this is no longer the case. Because the playing field is more "level" than it has ever been, how customers think about suppliers and their expectations for suppliers have become geometrically more exacting and rigorous. In this new world of available data and metrics, "good enough" no longer is good enough for today's customers. By necessity, suppliers have had to adopt an understanding of the "new consumer" that accounts for these new operational realities.

The new consumer retains an extremely high standard for relevancy in all of their interactions with suppliers, who must continually be positioned to answer the question, "How does this (product/service offering, etc.) help me now, and in the future, with these specific aspects of my business?" Customers have a reasonable expectation that suppliers will be able to answer this question—because the quality and level of competition for their business is higher than it ever has been in the past. The experiences that customers have—the nature of their transactional exchanges and interpersonal interactions—also have become an integral part of the adoption equation. Customers not only have an increasingly stringent set of baseline technical expectations, but they also now retain expectations pertaining to "bedside manner" as well. Long gone are the days when a highly qualified technical expert can talk over the head of a prospective customer, and expect to woo them with a whirl of details, difficult-to-understand specifications, and future performance outcomes. Today, a certain degree of romance is required in order to provide customers with the right kind of buying experience. Metaphorically, in the good old days a hamburger in the car would suffice. Today steak and a white tablecloth are just par for the course—and following our metaphor it takes flowers and candy as well.

Customers increasingly expect to have a great deal of attention paid to both to their questions and concerns, but also to their needs and wants as well. Because the market has become so competitive, there are always other suppliers out there who will lavish attention on an account if that's what's needed. Customers will not be ignored, or they will go elsewhere, taking their business with them. The bar with respect to how much time and energy each customer requires also has been raised. This is why it is essential for customers to understand—and to be helped to understand in very explicit terms and in a systematic way—how you will provide them with value. Translating the attributes of your products and services into a value statement that will resonate with increasingly sophisticated customers requires both a deep and current knowledge of your own offerings, as well as with the nature of your prospective (and current) accounts. Only by acquiring and applying this kind of pervasive, sophisticated bilateral knowledge can value be expressed in an effective way.

Not surprisingly, customers also want to be treated in a unique or personalized fashion that reflects their own set of distinct characteristics and individuality of purpose and focus. It is less relevant to you, tactically, to supply products and services to 10 businesses with identical patterns of operation and functionality than for each of these accounts to feel as if you think about their business as being, for all intents and purposes, exceptional. Customers want to feel as if you see them in this way, that you explicitly recognize that they are special, and that you treat them accordingly. Effectively transmitting the sentiment that you view each customer as unique is critical for the maximization of CLV, even if your in-house operations, logistics, and service won't necessarily change as a result; it's about framing.

Customers also want you to cut through all of the jargon and technical opacity that keeps them from fully understanding exactly what they're buying, how it will be supported, and ultimately what it means to do business with you. As a supplier, entrenched in the manufacture and distribution of your own products and services, the potential is there to take a great deal for granted when communicating with external stakeholders—be they current or prospective accounts. These stakeholders are not as experienced with what you do and how you do it, and as a consequence their ability to understand everything you communicate with them is extremely limited. You must be able to decode the inherent complexity embedded within the boundary-spanning transactional processes necessary for you to do business. If not, you will be at a disadvantage relative to other suppliers better equipped to communicate with customers at their own level of knowledge and familiarity.

Correlated with knowing how to effectively navigate discussions involving complex products and services is the issue of intentionally or deliberately attempting to mislead or confuse customers. Most customers—or potential customers—are savvy enough to realize some of their own limitations. They recognize that there are things they don't understand, particularly about possible solutions to their problems, and how these might align with their current business model. However, they know the subtleties of their own business in a way that you don't. When insufficient homework has been done to really flesh out a coherent or genuine value statement, there is a strong temptation to prevaricate or stretch the truth as to the nature of the benefits or ease-of-use associated with a potential solution. It is better to frame an incomplete (or underresearched) response with an "I'll get back to you on that" or "I'll have my numbers guy check into that" than present an unsound—or even potentially dishonest—affirmative statement such as "We can do that" or "We can get that done for you." Honesty and being prepared is always the best policy; customers burned once will turn to other suppliers who they perceive as less likely to deliberately mislead them.

Today, almost any kind of data or information is instantly and easily available on the web. However, there is a premium on the respectful handling of core operational and financial data pertaining to customers and to their business. The safeguarding of sensitive transactional or financial data isn't a luxury; it is a central, foundational expectation that all customers retain in the midst of their dealings with suppliers. This often plays a role in the decision criteria to go with one supplier or another. In the hypercompetitive, hyperconnected business environment in which suppliers operate today, maintaining a pristine respect for the privacy of accounts—and effectively communicating that respect in a range of ways—is essential for gaining and for keeping business. A reputation for the mishandling of sensitive data and client information can represent a death sentence for suppliers.

Finally, the "new customer" both wants and expects that their current and future problems and needs will be addressed by suppliers in an expedited and comprehensive fashion. Any kind of substantial lag between the emergence of a problem and a proffered solution—or even hypothetical solution—sends a poor-service-quality signal for which customers have an extremely low tolerance. Whether contractually bound or not, suppliers should be positioned to quickly locate detailed and extensive information and technical specifications directly pertinent to customers' interests, and effectively package and transmit this information in a timely way. This kind of attention to the problems and needs of the customer has become a baseline expectation that in real terms can be the difference between extra bases and a foul ball.

Effective Customer Relationship Management

It has likely never been more important to develop and systematically implement a system to effectively deliver *bedside-manner* service throughout all phases of the customer interaction cycle. However, there are several extremely prevalent inhibitors that can limit the effectiveness of the best customer relationship management—or CRM—process. These inhibitors take on four distinct forms—cultural, economic, linguistic, and temporal—and can produce negative effects on CRM.

Although there will be temptation to ask "Did you really just write that?" after reading our treatment of the first inhibitor, "cultural," what is clear from years of research is that most companies *really don't care* about their customers! Dealing with a customer is extremely time consuming. They can be finicky, unpredictable, difficult, demanding, and (from a supplier's perspective) disloyal. As a matter of corporate culture, many suppliers approach customers and their interactions with customers as a proverbial "necessary evil." In light of the costs associated with generating business, this thinking is both wrong-headed and also reflective of substantive misunderstanding of the accrual of "value." The fact remains that whether a particular customer's business thrives or not isn't really of great concern to most suppliers, who tend to adhere to an increasingly anachronistic *volume perspective*. In order to increase the sophistication of the customer relationship management processes—and by extension CLV—it is essential that the firm make a fundamental shift in corporate culture toward a "modern" view of customers that is more in line with their own self-view—valuable, valued, corporate partners.

The second inhibitor of the customer relationship management processes is economic. The well-worn adage that "you have to spend money to make money" is just as true as ever. It is especially true when it comes to investment in customer relationship management. Effective customer relationship management doesn't happen by accident, and it doesn't happen with luck. CRM requires investment spending just as with any other essential function or strategic core infrastructure. However, because customers are often seen as being peripheral in many ways by suppliers, the value of investment in customer relationship management isn't as salient to decision-makers as is the value of investment in other resources. In order to get good at managing relationships with customers, suppliers must be willing to make investments in both the infrastructure and the change management that can support this process.

The third inhibitor of effective CRM is linguistic. Although at first blush this may seem unlikely, it is important to consider this issue within its context—that is, within the context of interactions with customers. By necessity, businesses develop idiosyncratic language and acronyms to create efficiencies across a wide spectrum of activities. At UPS, a driver is called a driver service provider or DSP, a morning meeting is called a "prework communications meeting" or PCM, and a truck is called a "package car." This kind of language—at UPS and everywhere else—creates an internal cadence and familiarity that enhances the flow of ideas between insiders tasked with tactical implementation. However, what it also does is create communication barriers when communicating with external stakeholders in boundary-spanning contexts. Often, this is a beneficial, indirect consequence, except when interacting with customers. Customer relationship management is fraught with so much jargon and so many acronyms—OLAP, data warehousing, ERP, P-CRUM, drilling down, WAP, ADRI—that confusion is almost an explicit extension of this process. Customers exposed to this kind of swirling blow of jargon are not only unlikely to be left with feelings of having been treated in accordance with their expectations, but are more likely to carry away strong feelings of discomfort and alienation.

The fourth impediment to customer relationship management, temporal, is inhibited by the perspective adopted by decision-making executives. Squeezed by customers', shareholders', and stakeholders' expectations, executives and decision-makers down the line tend to adopt a short-term vs. a long-term perspective as they pursue "value." This quick-volume perspective incorporates as an explicit element a percentage-focus, and frames customer value as a probabilistic function. Like a lottery ticket, each customer or potential customer retains in aggregate terms a minimal value, because the ultimate chances of long-term success or value with each customer from this perspective is low. In contrast, the value perspective takes the opposite tack. Here, customer value is framed in more individualistic terms as a consequence of preselection establishment of fit (or congruence) between the customer and supplier.

Adoption of a short-term perspective mitigates any potential value from investments in CRM, because customers represent an essentially expendable commodity. In contrast, adoption of a long-term perspective explicitly recognizes that each customer has the potential to be—in and of itself—a foundational partner. Unfortunately, in businesses that don't adopt the long-term perspective, active engagement in CRM is seen as a luxury.

The Three Buying Phases and Intraphase Fluctuation

Although the nature of customers (and prospective customers) is continuing to change in the face of an increasingly competitive market environment, the process that leads to the decision whether to buy, how much to buy, when to buy—and from whom to buy—has remained fairly static. This predictable cycle emerges through three interrelated phases as you see in Figure 6.1. Through these three phases—Phase 1 where needs are determined, Phase 2 where alternatives are evaluated, and Phase 3 where risk is evaluated—we see shifting patterns across four critical decision criteria: needs, risk, solution, and cost.

In Phase 1, customers perceive a problem—a deficit of some kind—that requires an external intervention in order to be addressed. This is reflective of their perceived need. In this phase, the perceived need serves as a catalyst for action that leads customers to seek out a solution or solutions to their problem. The perception of need is at its apex in Phase 1, while considerations of risk and the particular aspects of the solution-in-focus are less central. Customers aren't necessarily focused on the specific aspects of the mechanism that will solve the problem, or the potential risks associated with a particular solution vector—but the need is there. Issues of cost also are central, but less so than the recognition of an unmet need, and decreasingly so moving into Phase 2, where customers evaluate alternatives.

Once a need has been recognized, and the decision to "act" has been taken—calls made, meetings set up, and so on—the primacy of the specific need itself begins to decrease in salience (or importance). In Phase 2, this is replaced by the particulars associated with the range of solutions in consideration. In this phase, the need per se has become an element of the decision-making background, while determining which solution is most likely to effectively address the need takes center stage. In this deterministic phase, where systematically fitting the specifications of the problem to the specifications of the solution is paramount, the issue of cost also becomes less salient to customers who are seeking an "answer." However, as customers consider the range of potential alternatives available through a range of vendors, considerations of risk begin to increase, reaching their zenith in Phase 3 where buyers are focused almost exclusively on risk.

In Phase 3, the particulars of the solution itself become less salient. Buyers have begun to frame the approach to their problem around a particular solution, and so its specific characteristics (relative to the other potentially available solutions considered in Phase 2) are less immediately relevant. Issues of price, however, become more salient as cost issues bear directly on the perceived risks associated with a particular vendor. These shifting patterns in buyer focus across the three phases of the buying cycle are predictable. This regularity represents a powerful lever. As a consequence of their regularity—or standardization of profile—these shifting foci can be addressed in tactical ways that coincide with the changing nature of customers and their expectations. Suppliers who recognize that customers go through a predictable set of cognitive and emotional responses as the decision to "buy or not to buy" emerges, and matures, can position themselves to respond to these responses tactically. This increases the likelihood of a favorable purchasing climate. Effectively utilizing CRM processes in concert with these predictable phases can further enhance transactional percentages.

Figure 6.1. Shifting Buyer Concerns

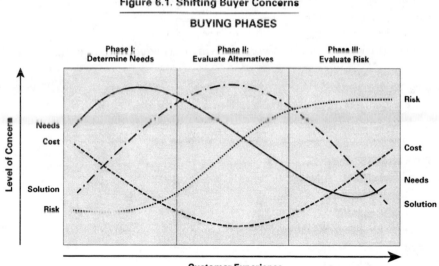

How Do We Respond to the Different Stages in the Buying Process?

Phase 1: Determine Needs

Order of Customer Concerns: Needs → Cost → Solution→ Risk

Reduce needs concerns through:

- Keeping the customer's perspective in mind
- Delivering tailored value propositions
- Being dynamic and evolving the message based on specific needs
- Anticipating objections and concerns
- Providing limited choice, specific issues of importance
- Keeping the sales interaction more about function and less about emotion

Reduce cost concerns through:

- Better information and reduced uncertainty
- Elimination of duplicated processes
- Better flow of supplies
- Improved supply chain efficiency
- Tighter quality control
- Reduced production and R&D costs
- Lower sourcing costs

Phase 2: Evaluate Alternatives

Order of Customer Concerns: Solution → Risk/Needs → Cost

Reduce solution concerns through:

- Moving more toward emotions and function
- Aligning communications and operations facing the customer
- Explaining how your offering fits into the larger supply chain
- Uncovering latent (hidden) issues that you can help address
- Taking a broader view of the customer's operations and what you can do to help
- Becoming a consultant in their business

Phase 3: Evaluate Risk

Order of Customer Concerns: Risk → Cost → Needs→ Solution

Reduce risk concerns through:

- Be transparent in the process of what happens after the sale
- Share long-term vision
- Keep a global focus
- Commitment to service
- Flexibility in approach
- Similar or complementary values
- Product/market differentiation
- Shareholder value creation
- Attainment of marketing and production objectives
- Willingness to share information and ideas
- Readiness for risk taking and sharing of costs
- Demonstrated commitment from both sides

Goal Setting

Across the spectrum of business activities that salespeople engage in regularly, setting goals may be among the most critical for effective tactical engagement and execution of customer-focused activities. Goal setting is a fundamental organizational process. It helps sales managers to direct their time, energy, effort, and personal resources effectively; identify key salesperson activities; establish and facilitate the demonstration of specified, strategically relevant levels of performance; generate connections between training, compensation, and performance evaluation activities; and motivate salespeople. Here we will touch on different types of goals, and how they impact the CRM process.

Cascading Goals

Because they are crucial for the enactment of firm strategy, goals don't tend to emerge on the frontline, or at the regional level or in an isolated or random way. Rather, the nexus of the goals that sales managers adopt, and that shape and drive salesperson behaviors, tend to emerge from the strategic imperatives identified by corporate-level executives, which "cascade" down through the organization and across organizational levels. Beginning in the C-Suite, one "Grand" goal reflecting a long-range vision is widely disseminated across all of the executives and managers who lead the tactical implementation of firm strategy. This "Grand" goal is then translated into a few new "Strategic" goals. These resonate in different ways with different managers in different regions, across different product/service lines, in different markets.

Although the "Grand" goals provide a broad point of departure, the "Strategic" goals that emerge take on some of the idiosyncratic characteristics of distinct areas within a firm where they emerge. From these few "Strategic" goals, many tactical or operational goals result. These operational goals represent the mechanical instantiation of the delineated strategic goals from the previous, higher goal-setting level. Finally, because they encompass an explicit operational focus, these tactical goals translate into a series of tasks or projects that service the "Grand" goal established at the highest organizational level. This cascade from the upper levels of management to the frontline activities creates greater strategic cohesiveness between firm direction and what actually happens on the ground with regard to customer-focused activity.

SMART Goals

In order for goals to be functional, they also need to be SMART. This is an acronym we introduced in chapter 1 to frame goals that are specific, measurable, achievable, realistic, and timed. Specific goals attach verifiable, numerical values to goals. Anchoring goals in this way provides knowledge of whether the goals have been reached or not. Goals which are Measurable provide a mechanism to verify whether the goal has been met. Measurable goals expedite tracking progress and goal focus. Achievable goals are reachable. Goals that are within reach encourage effort toward their achievement. Realistic goals are consistent with other strategic priorities. Realistic goals work in concert with other organizational goals because they orbit the same tactical imperatives. Finally, Time-based goals offer an explicit horizon for achievement; often accompanied by a series of milestones enabling the visualization of progress over a specified period of time, and a timeframe for goal achievement.

Goal Considerations

A range of goal "considerations" plays a role in both their enactment, and salesperson focus in their approach. Goals can be either personal or customer-focused. Personal goals may pertain to issues such as self-development, hours spent on work-related tasks, time management, and scheduling efficiency. Customer-focused goals, in contrast, may focus on factors such as retention, derived value, and product/services spectrum. These distinct foci influence the nature of the resources allocated toward their accomplishment.

Across these foci, goals also can be either micro or macro in their orientation, which carry inherent distinctions in arc-of-achievement tactics and timelines. Micro-focused goals may be accomplished within a day or two, and orbit events such as lunch with a potential client, a planned meeting with a distributor, or passing a certification exam for a new product category. Macro-focused goals, in contrast, are by definition more involved, with more moving parts, and have a longer horizon. These may include identification of new sourcing options within a product space, or building out and updating a decaying distribution infrastructure.

Finally, it also is critical to consider goal difficulty and articulation. If a goal is achievable 60 percent of the time, for example, it means that a significant percentage of the time the goal may be left unmet. If it is positioned as achievable a "majority" of the time, salespeople are more likely to view it as within reach. Effort invested to achieve goals follows a predictable pattern, typified by what is known as the "inverted U-shape." When goals are too "easy"—when percentages rise to 70–80 percent—this decreases effort as these goals are inherently unchallenging, because almost everyone can meet these goals most of the time. In contrast, when percentages drop to 15–20 percent, this also can decrease effort as they are too challenging—"most" sales reps are left with little to show for their effort. In contrast, when goal difficulty reaches a sweet spot—near 60 percent or so—this represents an apex in level of difficulty. Accordingly, the goal must be challenging enough to be stimulating, but not "too" challenging where it becomes demotivating and decreases adaptive selling. Goals represent an aspirational space—if no one or everyone is in this space (or can be in this space), they are no longer aspirational.

Goal Shaping

Goal shaping plays a central role in increasing employee effort toward the achievement of tactical initiatives and the pursuit of opportunities available for both employee performance improvement and potential maximization, as shown in Figure 6.2.

Sales managers who adopt a sequential approach to goal shaping explicitly recognize the importance of "present performance" as a baseline against which to drive future performance expectations. Initially, with a focus on present performance, it is important to set relatively easy goals with only small expected changes. Small wins can increase employees' sense of performance efficacy. Their sense of their own ability to do well increases employees' enthusiasm for increasing their performance.

Once this experience has become entrenched, and employees' enthusiasm for performance improvement has been whetted, the introduction of "intermediate" goals with larger changes can further catalyze this process. Over time, these larger changes and increasing levels of performance become the "new baseline" against which performance means can be visualized. Finally, as the performance climate becomes more mature, it is possible to introduce "perfection" goals—with only very small or incremental changes. Perfection goals become a long-term baseline against which "permanently changed" sales reps' performance is gauged and incentivized in order to drive strategic change. The performance and expectations of these "perfection-focused" reps also becomes a model for new salespeople, as well as a tool for sales managers who can point to them and say "Look at these folks—they did it, and so then can you!"

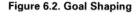

Figure 6.2. Goal Shaping

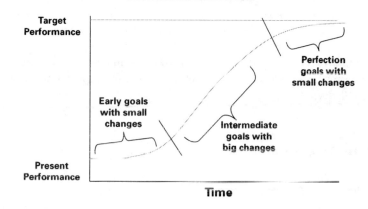

Evaluation

In order to serve as a means to encourage increased effort and motivation, explicit within the goal-setting process is evaluation toward goal achievement. The evaluation process is a powerful tool that, when used effectively, can continue to enhance motivation and effort over extended periods of time. To work, evaluations have to encompass observable outcomes that reps can easily understand, such as speed, accuracy, volume, or investment for example. The more amorphous or abstract the outcome being evaluated, the less directly impactful it is likely to be on employees' behavior or performance. In contrast, the more observable and measurable the outcome, the more likely it is to spur higher levels of achievement. It also is important to recognize that, although critical for execution of higher-level strategic goals, evaluation is a highly personal process. As a result, it is essential to have continuing member involvement in the process—from the setting of performance goals, to the tracking of progress, to establishing the most effective way to deliver feedback, to the implementation of performance remediation. Member involvement across all phases of the evaluation process increases the likelihood that reps will respond in favorable ways, even when the performance feedback they receive is less than stellar, or requires them to make changes in their approach. Development, guidance, and continuous improvement are inherent in any successful evaluation process.

It is critical we recognize that in order to be effective, feedback has to be given so as to allow employees to make actual changes in their behavior that matter. This means that the process cannot be limited to a once-a-quarter, formal sit-down with an employee. Employees have to be given regular, frequent progress reports so that they have the opportunity to modify their approach prior to any kind of formal intervention. This kind of continuing evaluation increases motivation, the likelihood that the process will lead to measurable increases in outcomes, and also retention—both of employees, who are more likely to stay when they feel they've been treated fairly, and of customers, who benefit from the process improvements derived from the evaluation process.

Finally, employees must understand how what they're being evaluated on relates to the strategic goals of the firm. Employees receive feedback better if they feel that there is a direct link between what their sales manager is telling them and the long-term health of the firm than if they feel that the process is driven by personality, biases, or differences of opinion (rather than fact). Within the evaluation process, there should be an explicit tie-in between strategic vision and the performance review. This strategic link also becomes more potent when reps are given insight into the relationships between their outputs (what they've done) and their outcomes (what they produce) vs. what they receive from the organization in terms of remuneration. This kind of explicit, mechanical insight further helps to motivate employees to continue to produce in ways that help the firm. As a functional point of departure, ultimately, unless the evaluation process leads to improvement in key performance indicators it will not serve the firm's broader strategic goals.

Key Performance Indicators

Key performance indicators (or KPIs) are a means by which firms can measure and monitor their own performance. KPIs are reflective of the processes or tasks that are central to delivering what the firm has defined as "success" for any given account or product/service line. Because of this mechanical relationship with established definitions of "success," they also serve as an underlying driver of salesperson behavior and actions taken in the service of tactical objectives. They help to quantify the firm's vision, and serve as a concrete manifestation of the actions necessary for the service of the long-term plan serving this vision. As with cascading vision from the upper echelons in the C-Suite to the ground floor where sales are made, KPIs also help to establish the parameters of the tactical goals that support the firm's strategic view by providing relevant performance measures and targets at the "local" level.

Benefits, Levels, Risks

KPIs offer firms several distinct sets of benefits. Because they are explicit and definite, they help to generate alignment across different units within the organization. They also provide a clear focus for both the development and the deployment of operational policy. Further, being operationally linked to the tactical implementation of strategic initiatives, they help in the identification of shared goals and objectives across all functional areas. Finally, because they ultimately are performance-driven, they serve as a mechanism for the establishment of operational baselines and benchmarks that can be used for goal setting, performance evaluation, and continuous improvement.

Broadly, KPIs can influence the channeling of scarce firm resources across several different levels within an organization. At the local level, from their explicit performance tie-in, KPIs can be used to monitor outputs and performance against a defined scorecard. Spanning boundaries, KPIs can also enable more effective listening to the "Voice" of the customer (VOC). The explicitness of KPIs facilitates their application in the monitoring of shared goals and objectives, both within and across organizational units and subunits. Finally, KPIs encourage active alignment to business objectives. However, despite these potential benefits, KPIs also carry several important risks. For example, to be of benefit, their use requires objective data—but the choice of which data to use has a significant impact on their likelihood of being effective.

The use of existing data which may not be relevant has the potential to lead to a systematic misalignment between enacted processes and strategic goals. Further, because the use of KPIs for decision-making depends on explicitly definable criteria, this introduces vulnerability to system-gaming or "cheating." Finally, there are implied, nontrivial direct costs associated with the collection, analysis, and dissemination of data for the metrics-in-focus. In resource constrained environments, these costs cannot be ignored in consideration of the potential risks of maintaining KPIs.

Criteria for Evaluation

In light of these potential and implied costs, it is important to develop a systematic means for establishing the criteria for the evaluation of performance metrics.

- The first is importance: Are you measuring the things that really "matter," given defined strategic and tactical goals?

- The second is ease: Does the measurement "flow" from the activity being monitored?

Whether focal data can be generated in a relatively seamless way or not has direct implications for the utility of a process that, to have an effect, has to be replicated multiple times, in a wide range of settings, across people and processes, organization wide. Once these questions have been answered, it remains to be seen whether the metric can initiate appropriate actions. If nothing can be "done" following the collection of KPI data, then the process becomes essentially an academic exercise with no direct functional consequences—or basically a waste of scarce resources.

Effectiveness or accuracy is a measure of how well enacted processes meet or exceed customer requirements. Effectiveness can be "operationalized" through the evaluation of defects, complaints, billing accuracy, one-touch transactions, and so on. At the other end of the performance spectrum, efficiency or speed of enacted processes is a measure of resource utilization. Efficiency can be operationalized as cost per transaction, time per process step, number of staff per process step, or bill of materials per process step. What these KPIs share in common is that both are of substantial importance—having direct implications for the achievement of broad organizational strategic goals, regardless of the nature of the sales process. Both KPIs are directly "measurable," and so determining their "levels" across a large number of transactions also can be accomplished within the flow of standard sales activities. Finally, both the effectiveness and efficiency metrics are actionable. They have direct implications for salesperson behavior, and can be implemented as a driver of process improvement.

KPIs also have broader strategic utility as a means to establish unmet market potential. Current—or recent—customer spending with a firm, which is an archetypal KPI, can be captured as an archived, historical pattern of value generation. These dollars are a matter of objective record, cannot be gamed, and are of critical importance for generating value and increasing CLV. Customer spending with all other suppliers in a particular category also represents, for all intents and purposes, an essentially objective measure of other-focused value generation, accruing to competing firms. Again, these numbers cannot be gamed, are of core importance to competitive position, and are reflective of current levels of market vulnerability.

Measuring the difference between customer spending with the firm, and customer spending with other suppliers in a particular category is reflective of untapped market potential.

Drivers of Purchasing Behavior

Customer spending and purchasing behaviors—with the focal firm or within category competitors—are influenced by a number of contemporary business drivers. As the speed of market change continues to increase, with an accompanying premium on process and operational flexibility, customers want suppliers who can provide creative solutions to their changing needs. In light of the fast pace of innovation and shortening product lifecycles, customers want suppliers who are positioned to help them get to market quickly, achieve wider penetration, expedite amortization of costs, and introduce new product development methods. Increasingly complex, emerging, and collapsing routes to market highlight the focus both on the simultaneous launch of new products and trial of new routes to market. In the face of globalization pressures, customers need suppliers who can help them reach global markets to maximize sales in the least possible time. Finally, and perhaps most importantly, customer purchasing behavior is driven by a combined focus on cost and risk reduction. Customers are looking for suppliers who can both provide reduced costs and mitigate risk.

Cost and Risk Reduction

Cost reduction can be accomplished through processes and structures that increase the quality of information and reduce transactional uncertainty. The elimination of redundant processes, enhanced efficiency in the flow of supplies and supply chain relationships, and tighter quality controls and assurance also diminish fixed customer costs. Cost reduction can also be accomplished though diminished or optimized production, R&D, and sourcing expenditures (from our discussion in Chapter 2 on CAN modeling). Risk can be reduced systematically through the combined influence of five firm-level processes: vision, culture, impact, intimacy, and balance. Customer risk can be offset with information transparency, by suppliers sharing their long-term vision, retaining a global focus, and adhering to a commitment to service quality. Flexibility in approach is a firm culture characteristic that ensures that customer needs will continue to be met, despite changing transactional constraints. Similarity or the complementary nature of supplier-customer values (or value congruence) also helps to ensure a long-term "fit" that diminishes customer risk. As we have highlighted throughout this book, the nature of the exchange between customers and suppliers has changed in fundamental ways over the last 15 years. Moving beyond selling to customers to helping them to achieve higher levels of competitiveness has become the contemporary raison d'être—or reason for being—for suppliers. Helping customers have an impact in their market, enhance their product differentiation, create shareholder value, and/or attain marketing and production efficiencies serves to diminish customer risk.

Willingness to share information and ideas and not being overly locked into customers' competitors reduce practical uncertainties and perceptions of risk. Another approach that can increase intimacy and also diminish risk is suppliers' readiness to adopt cost sharing or asset absorption strategies that spread liability across time and on both sides of the transaction.

Forecasting Essentials

One of the most effective tools available to reduce both risk and uncertainty is evidence-based forecasting. Different types of forecasts serve different operational goals. Market potential forecasts reflect the difference between what a customer currently spends with a firm and what that customer is spending with all other suppliers in a particular category. This difference is indicative of latent market potential. A market forecast, by contrast, plays a central role in market analysis, and is used to project future trends in a target market, divided into particular segments. Sales potential reflects the maximum share of a market that a particular firm "can" reach in a given period of time, while a sales forecast reflects the sales that a firm can expect to achieve during a given period within the context of a specified marketing plan.

The development of "useful" forecasts, those that ultimately serve the firm's long-term strategic goals, has to revolve around what might be thought of as tactical-push questions. These questions bear directly on factors that facilitate the forward progress of the processes implemented to execute strategy. These questions may have either an operational or a functional point of departure. For example, operationally, questions such as what time periods forecasts should cover and how often a forecast should be prepared provide a time horizon that binds forecasts within a particular temporal frame of reference. These questions link forecasts to established planning and scheduling goals. Questions such as who will be involved in preparing the forecasts, how will the forecasts be used, and what can be done to improve forecast accuracy provide an operational frame of reference that explicitly addresses resource issues both for forecast development and implementation. On the other end of the spectrum, from a functional standpoint, it is critical to answer questions such as:

- What types of forecasts are needed?
- What factors need to be evaluated in developing the forecasts?
- What data are available for developing the forecasts?

These questions are more "content" focused, and address, in specific terms, the functional outcomes of forecasting. Other questions of relevance concern what methods will be used to generate forecasts and who will use the forecasts, which we will cover later in this chapter.

Forecasting can be approached in one of two distinct ways. The first, as with cascading goals follows a top-down approach, while the other—with a local influence frame—follows a bottom-up approach. An inherent philosophical distinction across these two approaches is the issue of the direction of the causal forces driving sales numbers. When forecasting is approached top-down, the first critical element in the process centers around a holistic, comprehensive macro forecast of general economic and business conditions. This inclusive evaluation of general economic constraints then leads to an evaluation of market potential for a specific, relevant industry, which is contextualized against factors affecting the firm's share of total industry sales. This interactive evaluation of broad market potential and firm-specific limitations leads to an evaluation of sales potential for a company as a percentage of industry sales. This proportional evaluation then leads to a company sales forecast, and ultimately to sales managers' forecasts for individual territories and accounts.

In contrast, the bottom-up forecasting approach begins with individual salespersons' forecasts of specific accounts. Philosophically, the "account" is seen as the ultimate catalyst or driver of macro-level potential. Salesperson forecasts are combined and, as a body, are interpreted as territory forecasts. These territory forecasts are then combined and, again as a body, become district, region, and zone forecasts. Finally, these ultimately result in a company sales forecast. It is important to recognize that both approaches are valid, one implicitly embeds the firm and its sales potential within a broader—extra-firm—context, while the other implicitly embeds sales potential within a historical, within-firm context.

Things to Consider When Building a Sales Forecast

- Purpose and use of forecast

- Type of forecast needed (total sales, profit, number of proposals, etc.)

- Type of structure: top-down (determined by management and passed down) or bottom-up (determined by input from sales force)

- Who will use forecast

- Parties involved in forecast creation (see points 1 and 2 above)

- Time period forecast will cover

- Frequency of generating or updating forecast

- Data availability to generate forecast

- Technology's role in simplifying forecast development process

- Areas of improvement for forecast accuracy, speed of creation, and goal alignment

---

Collecting and Using Customer-Based Metrics

The majority of CEOs recognize that getting close to the customer is critical for any kind of sustained competitive advantage in today's hyper competitive marketplace. To achieve this, it's important to approach the collection of information about customers in a tactical way, and to be very selective about what kinds of information you're collecting. Collecting the wrong kinds of information can be misleading, expensive, and time consuming, and it can result in the misallocation of scarce resources and missed opportunities. Companies use several different approaches in the collection of customer-focused data. The first, which can be broadly categorized as falling within a traditional marketing metrics framework, focuses on assessing data across a fairly wide spectrum of variables such as market share or sales growth. These traditional marketing metrics offer a surface-level snapshot of the current sales environment, and firm position. The second approach, which centers on primary customer-based metrics, includes more focused-spectrum variables such as acquisition rate, acquisition costs, retention rate, survival rate, P (Active), lifetime duration, and win-back rate. These metrics undergird a more analytic, diagnostic customer-centric evaluation, and are reflective of customer behavior. The third approach encompasses popular customer-based metrics. These include share of category requirement, size of wallet, share of wallet, and expected share of wallet, and offer insight into the percentage or expected percentage of a customer's expenses that goes to the supplier.

Finally, we can look at strategic customer-based metrics, which encompass "value" in a comprehensive way. These include factors such as customer volatility, net promoter score, past customer value, RFM value, customer lifetime value, customer equity, and social network index. All four sets of metrics have their limitations but also the potential to provide us with important planning and health-related insight.

Market Share

Market share is a relatively straightforward calculation of a firm's sales relative to the sales of all firms across all customers in a given market. It is evaluated in percentage terms, where a higher percentage is reflective of a higher share of the market, and can be calculated on either a monetary or a volumetric basis. Although market share is one of the most popular metrics collected and used in reference to customers, there are several problems with its use as a means to drive tactical decision-making in an effective way. First, market share (or MS) provides no insight as to how sales are distributed across customers. This may hide problems with customers in terms of dissatisfaction or customer churn. Market share also has the potential to hypnotize a firm, particularly if it is the leader in a particular market. An excessive focus on market share also can result in a reduction of gross profit margins either as a consequence of large discounts or excessive expenses made to sustain market share (as an end in and of itself). A myopic focus on MS can entrance R&D and diminish innovation, potentially leading to quickly outdated products and an ultimate loss of market share. Individual share of wallet also provides an important indication of customer loyalty. However, share of wallet does not offer any clear indication of future revenues that can be expected from a customer. Further, unless share of wallet is evaluated in conjunction with size of wallet, it offers only a partial insight into the most judicious allocation of customer-focused resource expenditures. This is important, as it is essential to recognize that these metrics function interdependently. Increased market share can be accomplished either by penetrating each customer, thereby locking the relationship, or focusing on value and selecting customers with larger wallets.

Strategic Customer-Based Value Metrics

Unlike market share, customer profitability history or value is a function of the total contribution of all transactions attributable to a customer during a given period (or periods) of time, less applicable discount rates. Because products and services are purchased at different points in time throughout the association with a customer, all transactions have to be adjusted for the time value of money. However, aside from offering a relatively quantitative or objective historical appraisal, past profitability provides no indication of a customer's future activity. The metric also does not incorporate the expected costs of maintaining the customer in the future. In contrast, customer lifetime value, as we've discussed in earlier chapters, is a prediction of the potential gross profitability associated with the entire future expected relationship with the customer. A range of models have been used to develop the CLV prediction, which is based on the net present value of anticipated future cash flows. CLV plays an essential function in helping us shift focus away from a quarterly emphasis on profits to an emphasis on the maintenance of long-term customer relationships and their sustained health. In operational terms, CLV can also provide tactical guidance to set upper-level spending limits for new customers. CLV is typically based on past customer behavior and as a consequence may ultimately have limited diagnostic value for future decision-making. However, because of its long-term profitability focus, it may be the best tool we have to improve customer selection and lead to better resource allocation decisions.

Maximizing lifetime value doesn't happen randomly, or by accident. It requires an essential shift in focus. Increasing sales volume (through differentiation) and increasing sales value (through upgrades) can increase future revenue flows from each customer. Increasing efficiency and decreasing communication, distribution, transaction, and product expenses can improve future expense flows to each customer. Increasing the value offered to customers, by customizing products and increasing satisfaction and loyalty, can also play a central role in maximizing lifetime value. Finally, at the point of inception, from our focus on CAN modeling in earlier chapters, better prospect targeting can decrease customer acquisition costs, all of which can increase a firm's customer equity.

Customer equity is another metric used to measure value. It is a reflection of the sum of the lifetime values across all of a firm's customers. It is an indicator of how much the firm is worth at a given point in time as a consequence of the firm's customer management efforts. Customer equity, a metric used by some of the most profitable firms today, including FedEx, IBM, Netflix, Amazon, and eBay, can be linked to future company sales and the company's shareholder value. As an index, customer equity approximates market value, and is driven by three underlying building blocks: value equity, brand equity, and relationship equity. Value equity is the customer's objective assessment of the utility of a particular brand, based on perceptions of transaction costs associated with its acquisition. Brand equity is the customer's subjective or intangible assessment of a brand, above and beyond its objectively perceived value. Lastly, relationship equity is the tendency of a customer to remain loyal to a brand, for reasons above and beyond the customer's objective and subjective assessments of the brand. Firm resource allocations directed toward processes that can influence product quality, distribution, and price can have a positive impact on value equity. Resources directed toward improving brand awareness, advertising, attitude toward the brand, brand ethics, and CSR (corporate social responsibility) can be leveraged to improve brand equity. Finally, resources funneled toward loyalty programs and improved customer interactions can improve relationship equity. These three building blocks directly impact customer lifetime value and indirectly influence customer equity.

Examples of Performance Metrics

Traditional	*Customer-Value-Based*
Market share	Share of category requirement
Sales growth	Size of wallet
	Share of wallet
Customer-Life-Cycle-Based	Expected share of wallet
Acquisition rate	
Acquisition cost	*Strategic-Customer-Based*
Retention rate	Customer volatility
Survival rate	Net promoter score
P (Active)	Past customer value
Lifetime duration	RFM value
Win-back rate	Customer lifetime value
	Customer equity
	Social network index

Customer Portfolio Management (CPM)

So, ultimately, how does this all fit together? Finance theory tells us that the purpose of every for-profit business is to maximize its financial or shareholder value. This can be accomplished by maximizing future cash flows. Perhaps seemingly counterintuitive to the thoughts of our brethren in Finance, future cash flows are generated by customer relationships—not by products. So, even as we assess the collective value of our customers as a portfolio, the explicit focus must therefore remain on each individual customer, contextualized against their relative value as singular company investments in a much larger portfolio.

Each customer is evaluated against their economic/strategic value for the firm. The customer evaluation encompasses what the customer "expects" from the supplier (expense), and what can be expected by doing business with a particular customer (revenue). The supplier tactically manages the nature of the relationship that it has with each customer in accordance with the outcomes (predicted profit) from this evaluation, based on firm-level strategic fit. An essential aspect of this process is the development of the right kinds of customer metrics to measure value. The supplier develops tools for the evaluation of its customer base by combining a range of customer metrics. Understanding the individual value of each customer is paramount to determining the collective value of the portfolio, and hence associated resource allocation decisions.

Customers are then evaluated and segmented on the basis of the metrics that have been developed and applied a customer value, which drives both resource decisions and relationship management approaches. Customers are prioritized based on this evaluation. Consistent with the portfolio analysis process and techniques from finance theory, "important" segments receive more attention—and resources—than less important segments. "Optimal" resource allocations are allocated to each customer—communication, contact, sales, and service—based on their value to the company.

Call to Action: Actively Managing the Portfolio

After reading this chapter, you should be thinking about each of the customers in your portfolio, and specifically how their relationships add value to your firm. We now issue a call to action to salespeople, to identify the relevant metrics for each of these customers, as well how to forecast and capture the most value from each. Do you have the right KPIs? Do you have the right strategy? Are you focusing on the right customers? Use what you've learned in this chapter to drive your actions going forward.

Chapter 7

Key Account Management:
Planning, Strategies, and Blueprinting

"In marketing I've seen only one strategy that can't miss—and that is to market to your best customers first, your best prospects second, and the rest of the world last."

—John Romero

Rick Dinsmore, an account executive at Palmer Electronics, was facing a serious issue—maybe "crisis" was a better word. The economy had put a very serious dent in his budgeting and he was going to have to pull resources from several "B-level" accounts. He also had to decide whether to put money into a new inventory control tool to meet the tracking stipulations that TaiKack Distributors—a big client—had "requested," or to offer customization on a new integrated wireless package for Preston Technical Systems—also a big client. He wasn't sure if he could get both initiatives completed with the money he'd been able to scrape together. Even if he could, he wasn't sure how he would get them done or who he'd need to execute the initiatives on his behalf. He didn't want TKD to jump ship, which he felt was a real possibility if the tracking system didn't emerge, and he didn't want to lose PTS either, just as they were planning to launch their new wireless suite which would open up an entirely new market. He needed some way to determine where the largest returns were likely to emerge, and how to establish an approach to generate them. But how was he going to do it?

THE PURPOSE OF THIS CHAPTER is to pull together the many things we have discussed thus far and outline a process for account planning. We will follow the methodology for categorization of an account into the account portfolio, which will inform how objectives are set, how strategies are developed, and finally how to assign tactics to achieve account goals. The account planning process, for even the smallest customer or territory, instills a level of focused, systematic analysis and execution that maximizes the potential value of every account. The focus here is essentially on what is required to move an account from where it is currently to where you want it to be in the future. Accomplishing this involves a process—a process focused on generating account value through better research, targeting, insight, propositions, message, and tactics. The core outcome of the planning process is eliminating the difference between forecasted and actual value. The goal is to take the customer from where they are to where you want them to be. Because doing this requires planning, our focus in this chapter is on how to go about developing plans to move accounts—large and small—from their current to forecasted position, with a keen eye toward the cost-contribution ratio associated with the account. Account planning helps to provide the firm-specific calculations that are used to make decisions about investing resources into categories of accounts.

In a lot of ways, account management and planning is both "art" and science. In many underperforming companies, account planning is only poorly understood and only inconsistently applied. In high-performing firms, by contrast, account planning takes center stage within the sales process. The key driver of salesperson success is to understand exactly what is required to achieve "success" on every call made to an account. In most companies, 30–40 percent of all business is unprofitable, while the majority of most companies' profits are driven by 20–30 percent of their accounts. The quintessential objectives of all sales reps are to acquire the most profitable business possible, secure more of that business, and reduce less-profitable businesses. Given the continuing, central focus on the systematic development of metrics-driven, rational account valuation, and ultimately accurate placement within an account portfolio, the objectives for this chapter are to present a process for establishing account strategies and tactics that coincide with this analytic valuation process and offer a path toward the maximization of CLV.

We describe an approach to account planning that builds directly from the implications of portfolio development and account placement. We begin by describing the consequences of strategy, tactics, and the importance of appropriately defining both in accordance with portfolio position. We then outline the account planning process, moving from corporate strategy and marketing plan to analysis and categorization. We define account position, and the importance of tying these positions directly to appropriately oriented goals. We discuss account strategies, their nexus and expected outcomes, and tactics—their meaning, framing, and consequences. We then develop the link between account strategies and blueprinting, focusing on how strategies are built and their underlying drivers. We conclude with a focus on the blueprinting for accounts distinguished by their status as Strategic, Star, Status, and Streamline accounts.

Account Planning

It is almost a truism that all accounts are not created equally. Accounts can differ a great deal, particularly from the standpoint of their capacity to contribute toward the achievement of an organization's long-term strategic objectives. Some accounts are more strongly aligned strategically with the supplier than others, have a higher projected lifetime value, and are less risky than other accounts. Some accounts represent a higher level of current business than other accounts, consume a wider spectrum of products and services, and have stronger intangibles than others. As a broad statement, accounts differ, systematically, in terms of their relative levels of attractiveness and the strength the supplier has with the account. In light of these measurable functional differences, as we've highlighted in earlier chapters, it is critical to categorize accounts into like groups, differentiating them on the basis of the specific attributes that conclusively reflect their current and projected future value to the firm.

Once an account has been categorized using a range of relevant, quantitative metrics, the portfolio approach can serve as a guide that can be used to set objectives, develop strategies, and assign tactics that coincide with the value of the account to the firm. Actively utilizing the account management process, with even the smallest customer or territory, will engender the habits of practice necessary for achieving success when the stakes increase, and the potential rewards for successfully creating alignment between tactical approach and account value get really BIG.

Ultimately, account planning encompasses the process of actively moving an account from where it is currently to where you think it "can" be. Plans developed within this process should be focused on expeditiously getting the account into the forecasted position. The effectiveness with which account planning is executed depends both on the development of an effective strategy for the account and tactics for executing the strategy. If the strategy derived from the planning process is sound, and fundamentally solid tactics are formulated to operationalize the strategy, the account will thrive and its value will more quickly begin to reflect its forecasted value.

If the strategy is sound, but the tactics developed in support of the strategy are poor, the account will survive, but will likely never reach the potential value it has been forecasted to reach. The strategy is a critical—perhaps the most critical—element in account planning. If the strategy is poor, and the tactics developed to execute the strategy are also poor, the account will die a slow death. In contrast, if the strategy is poor, but fundamentally solid tactics are implemented in support of the poor strategy, the account is likely to die quickly! There is an old adage that applies here—if you don't know where you're going, then any road will take you there. As an extension to that adage, if you're going to hit a brick wall (i.e., bad strategy), then you'll hit it faster if you're driving a fast car (sound tactics)! A sound, rationally anchored foundation—strategy—is the essential precondition to maximize account value.

The concept of cascading goals has been used to understand the dissemination of vision and firm-level direction from the executive, or corporate, suite to the frontline sales personnel who move an organization's products and services out the door. Because they play a central role in the allocation of resources, the goals that drive the behaviors of sales managers—and that influence salesperson behaviors—emerge from the strategic goals identified within the C-Suite. These goals then matriculate through the organization, across organizational levels, becoming wider and more tactically pronounced as the goal is translated to each successive level within the organization. These goals ultimately emerge as specifiable tasks and behaviors engaged in by the members of frontline sales teams. A similar cascading structure of dissemination also is reflected in the account planning process. In account planning, a relatively diffuse, or broad, strategic emphasis ultimately emerges in the form of the concrete tactical operationalization enacted by boundary spanners engaged with the firm's accounts.

The Cascade

Account planning begins as an interactive combination of the imperatives implied by corporate-level strategy and a focused marketing plan. Corporate-level strategy reflects the overall approach taken by a diversified company. This approach bears directly on the firm's disposition as to the mix of businesses in which the company should compete, and the ways in which it should coordinate and integrate individual business units. Corporate strategy is the underlying mechanism that enables the firm as a whole to be a more effective vehicle for generating profits than would be possible for its individual constituent parts in isolation.

Marketing Plans

Marketing plans are composed of several underlying aspects that are in part shaped by corporate strategy. Market research, the first—perhaps most critical—aspect of a marketing plan, includes analysis of market dynamics, customer demographics, market segment, target markets, products, current industry sales, industry benchmarks, and suppliers. Once market research has been completed, it is possible to develop a description of your target market or markets, a description of the product/services in focus, and the unique selling proposition that will differentiate your products and services from the competition. A mission statement, identifying to whom you're selling, what you're selling, and your distinct value proposition in the market emerges from this process. Developing a set of marketing and promotion strategies that support your mission statement follows, leading to pricing, positioning, and branding approaches, your budget, marketing goals, and ultimately a strategy for evaluation of the results of your marketing plan, including hard sales numbers and customer feedback.

In conjunction with corporate strategy, the marketing plan facilitates the systematic analysis and categorization of accounts,[1] which is similar to ABC analysis in logistics management. In the categorization of accounts, or what may be termed selective account control, accounts are distinguished based on their importance to the organization. For "A" accounts, the firm keeps extremely tight controls, maintains extremely accurate records, and invests substantial resources because "A" accounts have an extremely high value and are disproportionately important to the firm, relative to "B" and "C" accounts. Their value to the firm justifies the investments made in the maintenance of "A" accounts. While "B" accounts are less critical to the firm than "A" accounts, they are still relatively important. Thus, while "B" accounts are less stringently controlled with less accurate records kept, and have fewer resources directed toward them than "A" accounts, substantial resources are expended in their maintenance and service. Finally, "C" accounts, which are recognized has having only marginal significance for the organization, are controlled using the least involved mechanism possible to keep costs low. Only minimal records are maintained and a very low level of resources directed toward "C" accounts, which in some ways are more an encumbrance than an asset to a firm.

In general terms, the Pareto principle can be used to understand the value derived from accounts categorized in this way. "A" accounts, which may represent only 20 percent of the firm's total account base, may generate 70–80 percent of the value the firm derives from *all* of its accounts as a body. The value the company is able to derive from these relatively few, critical, accounts is far outsized in comparison to their actual numbers. "B" accounts, in contrast, which may represent 30 percent of the firm's total number of accounts, produce between 25 and 30 percent of the value a firm is able to derive from all accounts. These "B" accounts are essentially at a point of equilibrium in terms of their percentage of representation and their percentage of value.

Finally "C" accounts may represent 50–55 percent of the firm's total number of accounts, but generate only 5 percent incremental value beyond that accounted for by "A" accounts and "B" accounts. Logically, in order to maximize ROI on the firm's accounts as a set, it is critical to understand from which accounts value is most efficiently derived, and allocate company resources in accordance with this derivation. From account analysis and categorization emerge an explicit evaluation of account position, account objectives, strategies for approaching the account, and tactics to instantiate these strategies, which is the logical sequence of events that ultimately leads to implementation of the account plan.

Position

Account position ultimately encompasses three elements that reflect on categorization within the firm's customer portfolio as "A," "B," or "C" accounts. The first element driving categorization is account attractiveness. Attractiveness is determined through an evaluation and summary of core account attractiveness factors. These bear on the account's ability to deliver value to the organization, and include the strategic alignment of the account with the firm's overall goals, the account's projected lifetime value, and the risk associated with the account. The second element driving categorization encompasses supplier strength factors. Strength factors pertain to the organization's ability to deliver value to the account, and include the level of current business the account is doing with the supplier, competitive standing of the supplier relative to firms offering similar products/services in the market, and extant relationship/structures in place with the customer. The third involves refining these factors into a value forecast for the account and the business implications of this forecast.

Objectives

Account objectives are a reflection of value goals established for the account. These objectives are tied directly to goals generated through forecasting, and are derived from the evaluation of the attractiveness and strength metrics determining account position. The critical consideration in the establishment of account objectives is an explicit focus on what infrastructure or resource deployments have to be *changed* or *maintained* in order for the account to successfully reach its forecasted position. SMART goals are used to evaluate the achievement of account objectives. As a rule of thumb, or broad approach strategy, it is typically most useful to generate no more than three objectives per account. Limiting the number of objectives in this way provides for a diversified set of success criteria, but also should help to avoid spreading tactical resources too thin—a consequence of objectives that are too broadly set.

Strategy

Account strategies are guided by the approach implied by the forecasted position of the account. Focal points of emergent account strategy may rest on considerations associated with product, price/promotion, distribution, communication, or information sharing. Strategies developed in the service of account objectives should directly lead to the changes necessary to achieve the forecasted account position. As a pragmatic operational criterion, for purposes of consistency, it is advantageous to employ one strategy per objective. This helps to streamline focus and offers a coherent approach vehicle. When more than one strategy per objective is established, it is more difficult to retain a consistent plan of attack vis-à-vis account goals.

Finally, tactics have to be established to facilitate the realization of the strategies conceived to achieve account objectives. Tactics are measurable, explicit, targeted, activity-based functions that, "on the ground," become the "who" and the "how" as to the implementation of account strategy. Tactics may be formatted and disseminated to key employees as a process map, or flow chart to enhance the clarity of the serial elements underlying the approach.

Tactical process mapping requires first establishing the boundaries of the tactical system that will be used to enact the strategy. These boundaries are established by providing answers to the question: "Where does the process begin and end?" The steps in the process then need to be defined, listed, sequenced, and diagrammed in a way that is communicable to key process actors—the sales personnel, support staff, and account managers responsible for the deployment of resources in the service of account objectives. In order to implement the tactic or tactics undergirding account strategy, it is essential to explicitly define system inputs such as information, people, machines, materials, and methods.

Once inputs have been defined, the process for transforming these inputs requires specification, as does the output—the outcomes or desired results (e.g., account change metrics). The final step in the execution of your plan is to stay in control of the process, continuously look for feedback both inside and outside the firm, and ensure that you remain aligned with your goals. Ultimately, each tactic becomes a measurable point of process evaluation. In order to ensure an adequate level of approach diversification, between three to five tactics should be developed per strategy. Fewer than this number of tactics may lead to an insufficient extent (i.e., points of contact with the account) of functional leverage to move accounts toward their projected status. On the other hand, when more than this number of tactics is deployed, this may lead to resource insufficiencies that ultimately impoverish the tactical set. Account resources are spread too thin for each tactic to be enacted at an adequate level of coverage.

Account Strategies and Blueprinting

Ultimately, once the value of an account to the supplier has been established, the question of strategy revolves around how you attack that account. What approach is most likely to lead to the emergence of anticipated value is the question that is answered at this point. Accounts' present day net value can be defined, in quasi-objective terms, based on historical performance data. Accounts' projected value is based on a combination of both art and science. The systematic, programmed interpretation of a range of available performance metrics leads to a forecasted value, which represents the anticipated, uncertain, future potential value of the account. The difference between the current value of an account and that account's potential future value is the key determinant of how the account is attacked.

Not surprisingly, the development of an effective account strategy, in light of subjective future value, is a fundamentally goal-driven process. The right account strategies have to be developed in order to meet your goals for the account. In order to develop the right approach, it is crucial that the strategy be as data-driven as possible, referencing current account placement, forecasted future placement, and account goals (revenues, products/services, category, etc.). In order to establish what strategic approach will facilitate the accomplishment of account goals, you have to answer two questions: What attractiveness and strength variables need to be changed? What type of blueprint can be used to catalyze the desired change?

Strategies

Account strategies are built based on a combination of philosophy and infrastructure, including strategic approach, manager competencies, and resource allocation decisions. We position ourselves to attack based on the account goals we've established. We employ the skills necessary to meet those goals, and we allocate resources using those skills. In the development of account strategies, from the A, B, C account evaluation process of determining relative account strength and attractiveness, emerge customers that fall into four categories.

Customers in these categories differ with respect to their utilization of suppliers' products or services, their relationship with the supplier, and their competitive status. As we see in Figure 7.1, the strategic approach, the managerial competencies, and the resources deployed in the service of accounts depends on their categorization as Strategic customers ("A" accounts), Star customers ("A"/"B" accounts), Status customers ("B" accounts"), and Streamline customers ("C" accounts). "Strategic" customers fall into a category defined by high attractiveness/ high strength—these customers coincide strategically with the supplier's goals and suppliers have high strength with the customer. "Star" customers fall into a category defined by high attractiveness/low strength—these customers align strategically, but suppliers don't have high strength with the account. "Status" customers fall into a category defined by low attractiveness/ high strength—these customers don't align strategically, but the supplier has high strength with the account. Finally, "Streamline" customers fall into a category defined by low attractiveness/ low strength—the account is not strategically aligned with the supplier's goals, and neither does the supplier have a strong relationship with the account.

Figure 7.1. The Decision Matrix

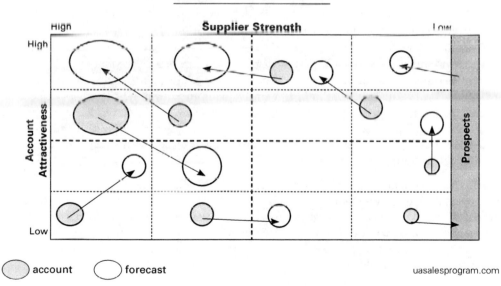

Based on historical patterns, Star customers underutilize suppliers' product/service offerings, maintaining only a basic or cooperative relationship with them. In order to reach strategic goals and eliminate the difference between current and projected value, it is essential that suppliers adopt an opportunistic approach toward customers, building business and points of leverage. The managerial competency most critical to the effective generation of value with Star customers is an entrepreneurial orientation, with an emphasis on the selective investment of resources to enhance market differentiation and expand the current range of offerings being consumed—moving them toward Strategic customer status. The strategic goal-in-focus for Star customers is to increase revenues and change their business focus.

Strategic customers, in contrast, make relatively full use of the available spectrum of suppliers' products and services, with an historical pattern of increasing utilization. The strategic approach most likely to enhance the probability of value maximization with Strategic customers is to build and to expand. The managerial competency most central to value maximization with critical customers is as a business developer to expand the consumption of current product and service offerings, and find new ways to increase consumption. In light of the core strategic importance of high potential CLV Strategic customers, heavy resource investments should be made. An exclusive focus on the expansion of product/service lines, with an emphasis on price leadership and broadened distribution, should be maintained in service of increased revenues and profits.

Unlike either Strategic or Star customers, Status customers are relatively unattractive. Although they generate revenues for the supplier, ultimately their business doesn't align strategically with the supplier's goals. Because of this strategic misalignment, suppliers should seek to either maintain the status quo with Status customers, or to reverse their strategic approach. The managerial competency likely to enhance the value of Status customers is managerial competence, which includes process or technical proficiency, the ability to coordinate resource decisions, and the ability to maintain organizational processes currently in place. Resource allocation in support of Status accounts should be maintained, or limits progressively imposed to reduce costs and increase profit margins. Suppliers should begin to eliminate unprofitable products, and stabilize prices, with a focus on profit maximization.

Streamline customers, which have low projected lifetime value (PLV), poor strategic alignment, and a nontrivial level of operational risk, don't generate a great deal of current revenue and are engaged with other suppliers. The best strategic approach to maximize value from Streamline customers is to manage for cash and regularly assess the relationship. Tacticians—or tactically skilled managers—are best positioned to wring value from Streamline customers, refocusing scarce resources toward other accounts. Aggressive elimination of unprofitable products and promotions, and increasing prices also improves value. Suppliers should withdraw from unprofitable businesses, maintaining institutional communication with Streamline customers, limiting information sharing, and maintaining profits.

Finally, Prospects represent a final category of relationships which have yet to be consummated—being potential customers. Neither their attractiveness nor their strength with the supplier has been established. Thus, the strategic approach toward prospects should be to subject them to systematic, quantitative evaluation. The managerial competency most critical to the generation of value from prospects is that of an explorer or investigator seeking out information, while resource allocation should be extremely conservative, leaked in the service of prospects. The primary goal for prospects is to create new streams of revenue.

Figure 7.2. Expanded Decision Matrix

	prospect	star	strategic	status	streamline
Attractiveness	none	high	high	low	low
Strength	none	low	high	high	low
Product/Service	unutilized	underutilized	increasing utilization	fully utilized	decreasing utilization
Relationship	none	basic or cooperative	integrated	cooperative	basic
Competitive	unknown	neutral to disadvantaged	advantaged	advantaged to neutral	neutral to disadvantaged
Strategic Approach	evaluate	opportunistic	build and expand	maintain or reverse	manage for cash & assess future
Manager Competency	explore	entrepreneur	developer	manager	tactician
Resource Allocation	leak	selectively invest	heavily invest	begin to limit flow	reduce
Product	targeted	differentiate & leverage	maximize expansion	begin pruning	aggressively prune
Price/Promotion	aggressive	aggressive for share	leader	stabilize	raise prices & minimize promotion
Distribution	targeted	controlled expansion	broaden to maximize	hold wide	gradually withdraw
People	single/institutional	account team/ institutional	account/ institutional/ departmental/ executive	account/ institutional/ departmental	institutional
Communication	selling	enough to overcome expansion barriers	strategic planning	begin to pull back	limited and controlled
Goal	create revenue	increase revenues	increase revenues and profits	maximize profits	maintain profits

Steps for Success: Account Strategies

Our emphasis in this book has been on approaching accounts in the most logically coherent way, given established account-specific goals. Ultimately, successfully achieving account goals depends on the adoption of the most effective account strategies for each type of customer, as summarized in Figure 7.2. How do you select the right strategies to adopt? Follow these steps:

1 **Setting the right account strategies to meet your goals requires determining the nature of the account.**

- Reference account placement and forecast: develop strategies based on available information.
- Reference account goals: be mindful of the account-specific goals.

2 **Setting the right account strategies will require answers to the following questions:**

- In light of account goals, what type of strategic approach will be most impactful?
- What attractiveness/strength variables must change to employ the strategy?
- What type of blueprint will be used to cause desired change?

continues

Steps for Success: Account Strategies (cont.)

3   **Employing the right strategic approach requires defining accounts accurately.** The type of account—Star, Strategic, Status, Streamline (and Prospects)—in focus drives the strategic approach, the manager competency, and the resources necessary to achieve account goals.

For Star Accounts

The Strategic Approach to adopt is:	opportunistic
The Critical Manager Competency is:	entrepreneur
The Resource Allocation approach is:	selectively invest

For Strategic Accounts

The Strategic Approach to adopt is:	build and expand
The Critical Manager Competency is:	developer
The Resource Allocation approach is:	heavily invest

For Status Accounts

The Strategic Approach to adopt is:	maintain or reverse
The Critical Manager Competency is:	manager
The Resource Allocation approach is:	manage flow

For Streamline Accounts

The Strategic Approach to adopt is:	surgical
The Critical Manager Competency is:	tactician
The Resource Allocation approach is:	reduce

For Pre-Account Prospects

The Strategic Approach to adopt is:	evaluate
The Critical Manager Competency is:	explorer
The Resource Allocation approach is:	leak

From this, the key takeaway is that logically deployed strategies are built based on:

- Strategic Approach
- Manager Competencies
- Resource Allocation

Ultimately, it is critical to remember that:

- We position ourselves based on account goals.
- We employ skills necessary to meet those goals.
- We allocate resources using those skills.

Strategic Blueprinting

A *strategic blueprint* is a comprehensive functional system designed to increase sales growth. The strategic blueprint is built based on products, price/promotion, distribution, personnel, and communication with customers. Suppliers give and take resources based on account goals, and use resources in combination to most effectively achieve value-driven objectives. The enactment of the tactics underlying account-focused strategies—putting strategies to work—is in essence of what blueprinting is. For any specific account, changing account attractiveness from a plus to a minus or maintaining a plus, influencing strategic alignment, lifetime value, or account risk, represents the steps necessary to enact strategy. Changing supplier strength from plus to minus or maintaining a plus, influencing current business, competitive standing, relationships and structures, also is central to the enactment of strategy. Blueprinting captures where a supplier will attack, how strategies will be employed, who will be held responsible for strategic objectives, and what contingencies are associated with a given tactic.

Account Attractiveness

Blueprinting for account attractiveness requires focus on strategic alignment, CLV, and account risk. Strategic alignment depends on the determination of the types of products/services the customer needs, in what markets/industries the customer operates, and what the customer's objectives and plans entail. The answers to these questions help determine where to attack and the strategies to use, as well as the core personnel and contingencies in place for enhancing strategic alignment. PLV depends on establishing the opportunities for entry/expansion, the severity of the obstacles for entry/expansion, and the potential bonuses/limitations to lifetime value. As with strategic alignment, successfully addressing these issues provides the foundation for decisions as to the functional parameters of approach tactics. Finally, account risk is a function of customers' current business climate, their competitive standing in the industry, and intangibles affecting attractiveness. These criteria then drive decisions about which tactics are most likely to close the gap between current and potential future customer value.

Supplier Strength

As with account attractiveness, supplier strength blueprinting requires the address of questions about its underlying constitute elements, these being current business, competitive standing, relationships, and structures. Establishment of current business levels requires determination of a customer's current level of product/service utilization and current service levels, as well as an estimation of current growth trends. How to tactically address the strategic goals for a customer given current levels of business depends directly on the answers to these questions. Competitive standing is a function of a supplier's competitive share of a customer's total supply, how important and sustainable their current competitive advantage is, and how important/reversible their current disadvantages are. These questions serve as a guide to the most efficient allocation of resources to address the proportion of a customer's business a supplier is able to successfully source. Finally, relationships and structures are defined by the strength of point-of-contact relationships, the strength of departmental and executive relationships, and capabilities for capital investment. These indicators provide a means to determine an appropriate tactical vector to adopt in the service of current relationships and structures.

Ultimately, successful account planning and the development of strategies to attack accounts successfully depends on an interactive determination of account position within the portfolio matrix and establishing tactics in support of these strategies that coincide with the value of the account to the firm. Because all accounts do not contribute value in equal proportion, effective categorization into strategic groups is essential for the development of account objectives and strategy development that agree with the value of the account. Effectively moving accounts from their current position to where they are forecasted to be depends on the generation of an effective strategy undergirded by strategy-bound tactics for its execution. If the planning-driven strategy is sound, and effective tactics are enacted, the account's value begins to reflect its forecasted value.

Steps for Success: Blueprinting

We have approached the issue of account management with an emphasis on the development of explicit tie-ins with the characteristics of accounts in focus. One of our primary goals has been to drive home the idea that the nature of the approach depends explicitly on the attributes of the account. The account-specific approach toward tactical blueprinting—which emerges from the answers to the 18-Question Diagnostic (from Chapter 5)—depends on the answers to the following questions:

Strategic blueprints are built based on:

- What kinds of products are in focus?

- What type of price/promotion approach should be adopted?

- How should distribution be executed?

- What people are necessary?

- What communication strategy should be adopted?

These questions require identification of the account-in-focus. When considering what needs to be done with each specific account, we must take the following actions for each account type:

For Star Accounts

Product:	differentiate and leverage
Price/promotion:	selectively aggressive
Distribution:	controlled expansion
People:	single to account team
Communication:	enough to overcome barriers

For Strategic Accounts

Product:	maximize line
Price/promotion:	share economies of scale
Distribution:	broaden to maximize
People:	single, team, institutional, executive
Communication:	strategic planning

For Status Accounts

Product:	prune unprofitable items
Price/promotion:	increase price and limit promotion
Distribution:	assess distribution points
People:	team and institutional
Communication:	begin to pull back

For Streamline Accounts

Product:	aggressively reduce
Price/promotion:	raise prices and eliminate promotion
Distribution:	withdraw from any unprofitable areas
People:	institutional
Communication:	limited and controlled

For Prospects (Pre-Accounts)

Product:	targeted
Price/promotion:	aggressive to test
Distribution:	targeted
People:	single or institutional
Communication:	selling

Call to Action: Strategies for Account Management

It also is critical to remember both that we give and take based on account goals and that to achieve great effectiveness we must use these approaches in combination with one another. In each of the previous chapters, and again in this chapter, we ask you to begin thinking about your organizational goals and strategies, and how they combine to serve your portfolio of customers. Again toward that goal, we are issuing a call to action to once again return to the steps for success. Ask yourself the questions. Identify and categorize each of your customers as Star, Strategic, Status, Streamline, or Prospect. Evaluate your strategic approach, manager competency, and resource allocation for each. Ask yourself if you have the correct strategic blueprint in place. If you do, improve it. If you don't, create it. Either way, this is a dynamic and continuing process.

Endnotes

1   Capon, N. (2001). Key account management and planning: The comprehensive handbook for managing your company's most important strategic asset. Simon and Schuster.

Chapter 8

The Role of Technology

"The real problem is not whether machines think but whether men do."

—B. F. Skinner

---

*R*ick stopped by the mail room during his only trip to the office this week. In his mailbox was a package containing the latest version of the most popular smartphone on the market. "This is the closest I get to how I felt on my birthday as a kid. I can hardly wait to use all the new features to help me stay on top of my business," he told a colleague from the accounting department making copies nearby. The response was a grunt, implying something much less than shared joy. As Rick tore into the package and began removing spare parts, instruction manuals, and instruction cards for the instruction manuals, his delight was somewhat dampened by a feeling of . . . déjà vu. This new toy, like its previous versions, will require him to visit the IT department to sync, download, and register the more advanced apps, and to input all the customer and competitor data and information that he never got around to putting in his old phone. Then, once all that is complete, it will take time to figure out how to use it to actually make a phone call. "What I really need," he said out loud, "is someone to focus on making my number for me this quarter so I have time to get this gadget up and running."

ONE OF THE RECURRING THEMES IN THIS BOOK has been the changing nature of the relationship between suppliers and customers. One of the primary drivers (if not *the* primary driver) of the changing market landscape hinges on the role played by technology in this equation. Here, we take a moment to reflect on the ever-changing, ever-more-essential role technology plays in the sales process. Our goal in this chapter is to build a "conceptual bridge" for the reader, illustrating how all of the pieces we have discussed to this point fit together as they intersect with technology.

The Services Marketing Triangle—Technology at the Center

While there is an ever-increasing reality that moves us toward incorporating technology into more and more facets of business, it is essential to understand the technologies in which you invest your time, and the specific roles they play in your organization. In a very fundamental way, salespeople are boundary spanners. These employees need to operate in a seamless way between the firm and the customer. Technology can play an important part in this critical boundary-spanning role. So . . . why a full chapter on technology? The purpose is to highlight other important areas for consideration, and the orbiting role(s) potentially played by technology. We do not seek to outline an approach for comprehensive technical understanding and adoption (which has been done extremely well in the book by Agnihotri and Rapp). Rather, here we offer topical areas in a sales architecture that may be bolstered by an appropriate understanding of where technology can be coherently integrated.

Figure 8.1. Services Marketing Triangle

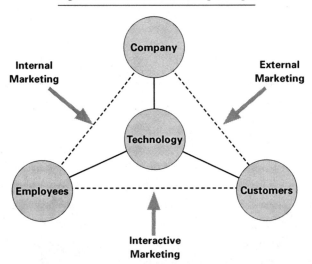

Zeithaml, V. A., Bitner, M. J., & Gremler, D. D. (2006). Services marketing: Integrating customer focus across the firm. Boston, MA: McGraw-Hill/Irwin.

Technology tools, systems, and applications are used to accomplish a wide range of core strategic purposes for organizations today. However, a smaller specialized set of these are relevant for the development and execution of a comprehensive, modern selling apparatus, these being:

1. planning and analysis tools.
2. communication devices and systems at both the firm and customer levels.
3. knowledge repositories and data marts used to capture and store codifiable information—and help us manage and articulate tacit-type know how.

Strategies to Tactics

Fundamentally, technology—and the use of technology—is tactical in nature. Technology, and the infrastructure that supports technology in firms, needs to be designed and built to support the initiatives that depend on it—be it at a firm or salesperson level.

It is commonly, or erroneously, assumed that technology acts as a substitute for capabilities. It does not. We all have a piece of gym equipment, designed to increase abdominal or pectoral strength, sitting in our basement collecting dust. We buy these pieces of equipment to enhance our health and fitness—but frequently this equipment becomes a laundry rack that goes unused. This equipment is only going to help someone who is already committed to push-ups and sit-ups—but it can't make you do these exercises. It can only help you get better results from the time you're already spending in pursuit of your fitness goals. Technology can be viewed in the same way. It is tactical because it is a capability-enabler that augments extant, underlying capabilities. Technology has to have a function into which it is integrated in order to be effective. If the drive to do sit-ups isn't there, if the capability is missing, then the Ab-Jacker isn't going to get you healthy. Just like learning a new sales process or trying a new technique, technology needs to fit into a larger strategic apparatus to have measurable benefits. The most expensive technology won't accomplish anything in isolation.

As the changing nature of the market continues to get more and more complex, the range of technological options available to decision-makers continues to expand. Today most implementations require a dedicated expert to decipher and decode all of the potential features and functionality that might pertain to firm- and customer-specific contingencies. Technology runs the gamut from, at one end of the complexity spectrum, proprietary customer relationship management systems, to the other end of the spectrum, commercially available mobile apps and voice recognition software.

Despite the levels of complexity, the purpose of any technology is to create a system that effectively integrates support for sales, marketing, and service across all channels and all products. For example, Salesforce.com has a number of application levels a firm can buy to fit the need of the organization. Thus the goal for any technology-aided integration is to create a single snapshot of the customer, as well as to augment the competencies of the personnel tasked with a set of disparate tasks and activities. Technology serves as scaffolding—facilitating the movement of raw materials and blueprints that undergird all aspects of the sales process. But, ultimately, for technology to generate worthwhile returns, it has to align to your approach—and must be integrated in a coherent, systematic way. Investments in support technologies that stray from this strategic, customer-centricity focus can only lead to disappointment.

There are a wide range of potential benefits—a long list—associated with the right kinds of investments in technology.

- Investments in technology can facilitate the collection and maintenance of the most current information and data on markets, customers, products, and competitors—connecting the firm with available electronic databases and up-to-date sources of industry intelligence.

- Technology can also decrease costs as it increases the efficiency of inventory and production management, or distribution and scheduling.

- It can improve communications, offering increased richness, flexibility, and security of real-time channels within the firm, to customers and supply chain partners.

- Technology can improve forecasts through sophisticated analytics software and data mining.

- It can improve management effectiveness by enabling more accurate and detailed data enabled performance evaluation, outcome metrics collection and analysis, and deployment of self-paced training modules.

continues

- Technology can improve margins by increasing the integration of supply chain partners and facilitating world-class inventory management and warehousing.

- It can improve sales effectiveness by offering salespeople real-time, in-depth customer analysis that can be leveraged prior to and during sales calls.

- Technology can increase customer satisfaction by increasing the sophistication of order tracking, delivery and scheduling information.

- It can increase revenues by broadening the range and scope of the firm's external selling apparatus.

- It can reduce administration costs through automated output and inventory control systems.

- Technology also can facilitate team selling by creating coherent, data-rich ties between the members of sales teams, the firm, and their customers.

As a broad statement, it almost goes without saying that if applied in concert with strategic trajectory, technology can fundamentally enhance firm competitiveness.

SFA and the Customer Relationship

Firms today have placed a great deal of emphasis on the application of technology to the questions of customer relationship and advantaging the sales force. While CRM—customer relationship management—technologies are used to increase both strategic and tactical focus on the management and capabilities associated with customer retention, SFA—or sales force automation—in contrast is used to manage and support sales reps' day-to-day activities. In broad terms, SFA encompasses the management of contacts, intelligence, opportunities, and pipeline. CRM technologies bring the customer into sharper focus. CRM enables the more effective view of history, the tracking and handling of inventory and relationship issues, order tracking, and customer support. In contrast, the focus of SFA technologies is on increasing sales, meeting the ongoing technical needs of salespeople, increasing close rates, and managing the daily mechanics of selling. Often SFA software is embedded in CRM systems, both of which utilize overlapping databases, but each retains a distinct focus—one is outward, one is inward.

Ultimately, it comes down to maximization of the *content-contact* curve, which is our model for speaking directly to a salesperson's unique ability to access both the customer and in-depth support information about that customer at the same time. Technology allows us to extend the content-contact curve enabling salespeople to have more access to, and to be positioned effectively to utilize more information about, more customers, more easily, more consistently, and more directly in order to touch them.

Using Data to Maximize CLV

As we've discussed earlier, in light of the nature of the competitive forces reshaping the markets that define the meaning of competition today, it is critical that firms consider a shift away from volume toward a focus on generating and increasing per-customer value. Of course, for some firms, in some industries, the entire story is based on standardization and volume—so this maxim clearly doesn't apply. But, where value plays a key role in generating competitive advantage, it is critical that technology be applied in the service of effective account management.

Maximizing customer lifetime value, at the portfolio level, requires deep insight into the nature of customers and their revenue generation capabilities relative to other customers within the portfolio. Ultimately, to have any kind of functional consequence, resource decisions driven by this systematic categorization require a data-driven analysis. Data can be used to profile customers and create discrete customer segments. Salespeople can then use information generated through technology-aided data analysis to predict customer behavior, and derive insights from information when making decisions regarding whether to grow, retain, or win customers.

CRM Failures and Challenges

Although technology holds immense promise with regard to the generation of increased lifetime value, its application and integration in existing firm-level systems requires an extremely careful hand.

Sales force technologies and customer relationship management applications have been touted as a panacea for nearly all sales force issues. But, it also is possible—and is borne out in the academic research in this area—that technology also has the potential to impede performance. For example, the implementation of certain technologies or tools may decrease employees' organizational commitment and job satisfaction, leading to increased absenteeism and voluntary turnover. This disturbing pattern of events lends credibility to what has been framed as the *productivity challenge* of information technology—which is that technology adoption and use may have unintended effects on productivity and may actually be detrimental to the achievement of performance outcomes. Several of these challenges are worthy of specific attention.

The Planning/Improvisation Challenge

We've explored technologies that can be used as planning tools, which can help salespeople, support staff, operations personnel, customers, other boundary spanners, and management effectively coordinate meetings and other social events. So, what is the hidden challenge here? The flexibility that this application offers is welcomed by some because it facilitates the generation of on-the-spot planning. Others find it liberating because it can eliminate the need to make plans in advance. But, overreliance on technology potentially becomes a substitute for planning rather than a tool to augment it. This can lead to a loss of skill to plan ahead or to make appointments in advance. When complacent, people can develop a shift of mind that in its extreme works against future-oriented or creative thinking.

The Engagement/Disengagement Challenge

Within an ongoing, hectic, daily schedule, technology provides its users with an alternative point of socialization. Without a doubt, it has an enormous potential to facilitate engagement. But users must make the choice when to engage with others who are present in their physical surroundings, and when to disengage and focus on their virtual points of contact. Everyone has the desire (which varies from person to person) to retreat from stress-inducing situations, while simultaneously remaining involved in the ongoing events in their life. Unfortunately, for most of us, it is extremely difficult to remain engaged in ongoing parallel activities.

Most people believe that we've become better at "multitasking," when in reality we focus on things more sequentially today than ever before. It tends to be very difficult for us to become engaged in a new task without disengaging from other tasks. When calls, texts, e-mail updates, tweets, and so on interrupt a conversation between people in real time and real space, this can often lead to abrupt disengagement of one party from the current conversation and engagement in the new one. When this occurs in a business context, everyone else previously engaged in real time and space is grounded. One of the reasons there are now texting-while-driving laws in most states is that we simply are not well equipped to engage in two complex tasks simultaneously.

The Public/Private Challenge

We tend to think of our mobile devices as tools that enhance our ability to effectively and conveniently engage in private communication with others, no matter where we are. Users of these technologies—all of us!—can very quickly establish a space within which to engage in what is, in reality, virtual communication in almost any location (bathroom stalls, airline seats, tables at restaurants, the coffee shop, the swimming pool, the library . . .) at any time of day or night. Because our communications are no longer limited to the home or office, and we've been emancipated from the conventional constraints of "wired" technologies, private communications are now conducted in public spaces—but, they may not be private. Anyone within earshot may be privy to critical details of your plans. Should these "plans" include sensitive business information, you may find yourself violating critical privacy clauses of your company or that of your customers, in addition to disturbing those around you.

The Illusion/Disillusionment Challenge

When we first see and then unwrap a present—before the box inside the package is actually opened—there is a point of infinite potential, of imagined possibilities, that is extremely fleeting. Once the package itself is opened, the possibilities and potential we just experienced shrink to more closely coincide with the object itself, and we are brought back down to earth. It is our imaginations that soar, not the objects we imbue with our thoughts and dreams. It is no different for salespeople when they first acquire a new piece of technology, or upgrade an older technology to a more current model or service package. Ah, the possibilities!

This process unfolds with a great deal of anticipation, enthusiasm, and excitement because of the potential we attribute to the experience, intensified by extensive advertising and promotion. Salespeople develop unreasonable expectations that this new technology will make their work easier, and enable them to achieve more than in the past. But, just as the abdominal machine gathering dust in the basement doesn't magically lead to a six-pack, salespeople often come away disappointed. When the realization sets in that the technology—like most anything that we purchase—delivers only a rough approximation of projected promises, the experience can leave one feeling flat, and demotivated to explore the potential benefits that the technology can offer. Salespeople should therefore quickly engage in the reality of the benefits and functionality of new phones and tools—to ensure that such expenditure delivers an element of the original expectations—in order to leverage the greatest performance improvement from the investment without disrupting normal operations.

The Empowerment/Enslavement Challenge

We are in love with choices and freedom to explore options. We don't like to be constrained or left without alternatives. One of the attractions that has driven the massive revenues associated with mobile technologies is the freedom of choice available to all kinds of users. There were almost universal accolades for the potential of these technologies to provide access to everyone and anyone through an "always on" mobile technology—and a system that facilitated continuous immediate access.

We were attracted by a permanent connectivity that would allow people to "be on" at any time, in any place, and for any reason, blending our work and personal information—beach pictures, work report, client meeting, soccer game, and fantasy football. This capacity—this freedom—empowers users. By the same token, however, the powerful technologies we carry around with us into the restaurant, to the soccer game, or to the bathroom prevent the creation or certainly the maintenance of distance from others. For many people, interacting with their mobile device has become almost a compulsion, distracting them away from their daily lives, and entangling them in engagements they'd just as soon avoid. It has become increasingly difficult to get away from our phones, tablets, connections and be where we are, when we are, doing what we'd been doing before the phone rang.

The Independence/Dependence Challenge

We have also moved into a phase in our collective use of technology wherein we've begun to rely on it more and more—remembering meetings, finding our way, buying tickets, making friends, and remembering phone numbers. Perhaps more relevant, the people who rely on us—our supervisors, teammates, customers, friends, family—use technology to connect with us when they need us. The mobile devices that people carry around with them every day, really, are seen as doing everything. We don't have to leave the soccer game to send out the e-mails that "need" to go out. We can pull up a spreadsheet and analyze data for our manager's meeting and send it to them while we're on the plane heading into town, where in the past if it wasn't done the night before, it wasn't going to get there in time. We can be reached for work at 20,000 feet, at the ballpark, and in the backyard. But, the power to remain connected regardless of historical constraints of space and time has led to the emergence of a new kind of technology-dependence (and some would offer anxiety). In some company cultures "being available" 24/7 is seen as "commitment." But, in reality it is reflective of the absence of independence—essentially creating an invisible, electronic chain linking us to everyone and everything else in our lives.

The Fulfills Needs/Creates Needs Challenge

Most people will agree that although we are able to get more done today than ever before, and have more flexibility in how we do our jobs than ever before, the full suite of available mobile technologies has also made our lives much more complicated than it has ever been. Although mobile technology offers a wide range of incredible solutions to problems that were unimaginable just 10 or 15 years ago, it has also introduced a whole new set of problems that didn't exist when wireless was a reference to eyeglass frames rather than how we communicated with one another. These problems can run the gamut from needing an apparatus to carry your mobile device, to having the right cords to recharge when your battery runs low, to not "having any bars," to not having compatible software, as well as a host of more substantial needs.

Here, in the space that is increasingly being filled by technology, it is becoming clear that our solutions have created a new set of problems—technology has fundamentally shifted how we think about what being a salesperson means today.

The Competence/Incompetence Challenge

The capacity to solve problems, create connections, analyze data, create reports, meet with customers, track inventory, price compare, conduct market research—essentially to do "anything" anywhere, anytime—has thus led to the emergence of a wide range of competencies for users of technology that would have been unheard of a few years ago. It enables salespeople to do a whole host of things they simply were unable to do in the past. Although it can and does increase both users' efficiency and effectiveness in accomplishing technology-enabled tasks and activities, it also can and does lead to feelings of incompetence. "Simple" processes and techniques are revealed to be more complicated than their surface functionality would suggest.

Efficiencies achieved through technology-enabled processes are sometimes revealed to be more difficult, harder to use, and more limited in scope for some people, and can actually decrease the emergence of higher-level efficiencies. That newly acquired technology-aided competence can diminish related competencies is a challenge that has emerged across a range of technology applications. The critical takeaway throughout this section is that the nature of the sales process is changing not in small part due to the technologies that increasingly define the nature of the markets in which we operate today.

Maintaining a clear focus on the customer and the sales process can help to eliminate some of the challenges associated with adoption and application of technology to enhance the potential efficiency of these processes.

Need a few steps to help overcome these technology challenges?
- Ask yourself, "Do I really need this technology?"

- If not, remove it from your life.

- If so, become the master of it.

- When possible, innovate with the technology you already have.

- Seek out help from colleagues, trainings, or online.

- If you have to use it or it will make you more effective or efficient, overcome the fear of the unknown and embrace the technology.

- Set boundaries for when, where, and why you will use the technology. Begin with small, quick projects that enhance learning. Find a technology partner and learn through "the wisdom of crowds."

Final Thoughts on Time
and Resource Management

As salespeople, educators, academics, and consultants, this book has been a labor of love for us. In many ways, it has been an expression of our (collective) life philosophy about what selling means today and how it can—and should—be done with maximum impact. We have been immersed in the sales process from every conceivable angle. We teach it, experience it, help others to do it better, and write about it both in broad strokes and in technical detail. We think about what it takes to be a better salesperson and to develop a better firm-level sales apparatus in much the same way that a trainer or coach helps someone to become stronger and fitter, and to achieve personal wellness goals. These are things that can be learned, and with practice and focus, mastered. These are not easy things to do, but there is a way to do them, and they are reachable, with work, focus, and diligence.

We have seen and continue to see the immense, transformative shifts that have occurred in the sales landscape over the last 15–20 years. These changes have forced us—have given us the opportunity—to think about our approach to selling, teaching, research, and training in new ways—constantly changing ways. These changes have coincided operatively with an explosive rise in the availability and applicability of affordable technological tools to facilitate conventional sales processes, tasks, and activities. Although we've noted the inexorable focus on technology, and that its use in the marketplace and the sales process carries with it some unexpected and potentially precarious consequences, for the most part the changes we've witnessed have led to a vastly increased clarity in the sales process.

Advancements in information, communication, and analytics technologies also have led to fundamental changes in our views of the customer, the expectations customers have with regard to the sales process, and the operational baseline necessary to be competitive in sales today. We need to be better, smarter, more informed, more customer-focused, more diligent, more prepared, more expert, more broadly knowledgeable, more flexible, more efficient, more prescient, and more persistent than ever in the past. The world is changing. The set of knowledge, skills, abilities, and other characteristics (KSAOs) required to develop a successful firm-level sales apparatus and to be successful in sales today is different from the set that was necessary to be successful 10 years ago—and will likely be different 10 years from now. The set of KSAOs could hardly remain the same in the face of an ever-changing sales landscape and marketplace dynamics.

As the nature of the marketplace in which salespeople operate continues to become more and more complex, forging a different breed of individual and organizing structure to be successful is critical. Salespeople, sales managers, and account managers have to be more sophisticated, intelligent consumers of information and its interpretation, application, and use than ever before. In the new information age in which we live, sales success or failure can be differentiated on the basis of competencies in these areas. No longer is being "Big-Joe-Brown-damn-glad-to-meet-ya!" enough to win all of the quarterly sales awards in a firm. Joe's second incarnation as "Mr. Joseph Brown, product expert, client expert, solutions expert" is much more likely to collect all of the hardware historically reserved for his backslapping, big-drinking, long-driving, big-personality forebears.

Budgets have tightened. Margins have shrunk. The game has gotten much more complicated (and more difficult) to play, and to play well. It has gotten more sophisticated on multiple fronts. But, despite what have to be characterized as crucial, structural shifts in the mechanics of the sales process that coincide with its increasing complexity, the elements underlying the development and maintenance of a successful, firm-level sales apparatus have not changed, and are unlikely ever to change—even by the time that salespeople are selling cargo space on the weekly space-shuttle to the moon. What we have taken from the cumulative experiences we've had in our ongoing roles, which annually put us into regular contact with hundreds of sales professionals from literally scores of firms in a wide number of different industries, is that the more that the status within which the sales process continues to shift, the more critical it is to retain a disciplined focus on the fundamentals of the process.

Sophisticated salespeople understand—have always understood and always will understand—that, in the end, their success ultimately depends on a determination of the best way to most effectively allocate scarce resources, and then systematically apply this calculation to maximize returns on their resource investments. It doesn't matter whether we're talking about selling livestock, feed corn, space on a cargo ship, passenger vans, tanning beds, dry goods, travel services, or advertising—different accounts carry different utilities. They always have and always will. The best salespeople understand that potential account value is differential and variable. They also make decisions that correspond with their evaluation of the value that can potentially be derived from any given account at a given point in time.

The best salespeople also understand that they have only a limited number of hours per day to do all of the things that they have to do. Time spent on the phone means time away from research means time away from sending a text means time away from making a new contact means time away from finalizing a deal means time away from family, friends, exercise, relaxation, training, development, and so on. The best salespeople understand, in a deep way, that the decisions they make about how to spend their time, by definition, mean that they've also *made a decision* not to spend time doing something else. They don't expend time by accident. They make decisions about how to spend their time in a way that corresponds with their focus on value. Here, to wrap up the resource question we develop throughout the book, with ideas from the beginning and the end of the book, we draw some comparisons between resource management and portfolio matrix scheduling and the prioritization matrix.

There is a difference between salespeople and great salespeople. These two groups are distinguished by their ability to make the right kinds of decisions, about their time and where it should be focused. Early on, we talked about the importance of being able to draw a distinction between the activities you spend your time on that are likely to have tangible benefits for you in the long term from those activities that just take time. Doing this requires the ability to understand your own priorities, and recognize the difference between those activities that bear directly on these and those that don't. Successful salespeople understand this. Putting first things first isn't a matter of luck or intelligence. It is a matter of disciplined thinking about what you are trying to accomplish—your goals—and drawing an explicit connection between how you spend your time and achieving these goals.

We talk to literally hundreds of salespeople every year. We eat meals with them, we socialize with them, we spend a great deal of time with them, we train them, we teach them, we share stories, commiserate, and we also learn a great deal from them—what they do, what they think, and how they approach their decisions. A very small percentage of these salespeople are what we thought of as the "best." Great salespeople have spent a lot of time thinking about where their time goes. They have also spent a lot of time practicing putting first things first as it pertains to achieving their goals. As academics and as trainers, we like to try to simplify the world. Although a lot of real-world complications inherently enter into the decision-making calculation, there are some fairly straightforward differences between what we should be doing now, and what we shouldn't.

From the perspective of achieving critical goals, there are activities or tasks that truly bear on their accomplishment—these are what we talk about as being "important" tasks. Important tasks matter, they have an impact, they are critical, they are central, they play a role, they have long-term substantive consequence. In contrast with important tasks are those that have a feeling of urgency associated with them. There is pressure attached to these decisions—sometimes it is a time-derived pressure, sometimes it is a socially-derived pressure—but these decisions feel pressing. It is critical to recognize that there is *no correlation* between the important tasks that you contend with on a day-to-day basis and the urgent tasks you face.

If you are not a careful steward of your time, all of it can be drawn into urgent tasks that take you no closer to achieving your goals than you were at the beginning of the day. The tasks that come knocking at your door, in texts, in voice mails, in e-mails, over Facebook, Twitter, or the phone that all carry with them urgency have to be examined—and identified as important, or not. The best salespeople out there distribute their time in a very different way than average salespeople. The best salespeople understand the difference between important and urgent.

They actually spend a slightly lower percentage of their time on tasks that are both important and urgent (20–25 percent) than the average salesperson (25–30 percent). This is primarily because these folks avoid allowing important tasks to become urgent. So there is a small (but significant) difference in the percentage of time that the best salespeople and average salespeople spend on important, urgent activities; such as crises, pressing problems, and deadline-driven projects. These come up, and have to be dealt with—but the best salespeople are more adept at keeping them from become urgent.

The biggest progress-forward distinction between how the best salespeople spend their time and how "average" salespeople spend their time can be seen in time spent on important activities that are not urgent. These tasks and activities are pivotal—they drive goals—but they are not pressing. These activities can be thought of as foundation-laying activities, and include, for example, prevention activities, relationship building, recognizing and preparing for new opportunities, planning, and sales and service training. These activities are goal accelerators—they really matter, and the best salespeople understand this, spending anywhere between 65 percent and 80 percent of their time in this quadrant. Average salespeople, by contrast, spend roughly 15 percent of their time here—missing the opportunity to develop their foundation.

The biggest progressive-regressive distinction between the best salespeople and average salespeople can be seen in the difference between time spent on important versus urgent, unimportant activities—the constant buzzing in our lives, including interruptions, some calls, voicemail, e-mail, reports, meetings, and popular activities. These can really be thought of as distractions away from the professional goals that differentiate the best from everyone else.

Top salespeople allocate roughly 15 percent of their time to these kinds of activities, while average salespeople allocate between 50 percent and 60 percent of their time here. From our experience, and from the available data, it is simply impossible to break into the upper echelons of the sales profession when so much time is spent in the service of unimportant urgency. When we allow these distractions to consume the majority of our time—or if we don't fight their inertia—their gravitational pull can drag us into a black hole where professional goals die. The best salespeople have been able to avoid becoming addicted to the urgency that can derail a professional career.

This framework offers a linear path toward a more efficient allocation of perhaps our most precious resource—time. The question of resource allocation, however, as we've tried to highlight throughout this book—is of core relevance across all of the levels of the firm where decisions of this kind have to be made, particularly with regard to the maintenance and development of accounts and the generation of value. As with the best salespeople, account planning is a firm-level differentiator of competitive advantage.

As with the character of the daily tasks and activities we are faced with on an ongoing basis, all of the accounts within a firm's portfolio also can be differentiated on the basis of charac-teristics that *should* drive the resource allocation decisions made in their service. The best salespeople don't waste their precious time on urgent, unimportant activities because doing so works against the achievement of their long-term strategic goals. Average salespeople are perhaps unaware that these activities are unimportant, because they haven't devoted their focus toward the development of a systematic understanding of the relationships between their daily decisions and the achievement of their professional goals. The best salespeople un-derstand these relationships, and are careful to expend their time in a way that most directly benefits them.

The portfolio structure within which accounts can be categorized—as with the framework for the management of time—offers a conceptual framework for planning how to deploy resources in the most effective way. Maximization of customer lifetime value depends on an understanding and systematic categorization of accounts into discrete bins based on two critical characteristics—attractiveness and strength. Doing so leads to a distinct definitional categorization that—once made—has a series of implications regarding resource focus, expectation, and relationships.

Suppliers have strength with Strategic customers who also align well strategically with the firm's goals. These customers drive business, and so the goal for these customers is to increase revenues and profits. But, the relationship with these customers is not particularly dynamic—this is a marriage, and so strengthening is critical, but change is less critical. The supplier has less strength with Star customers, who also align well strategically. Although increased revenue goals also are critical for Star customers, the fundamental imperative is on shifting the nature of the relationship. This is not a marriage. This is more akin to an ongoing romantic courtship with a beautiful partner, who has other love interests, but who would make a really wonderful spouse if it were possible to make this happen. These resources help to change the status quo.

The dominant focus of top salespeople on important, not critical tasks corresponds to the resource focus on Star accounts. Resources expended toward the evolution of Star to Strategic accounts can help facilitate strategic competitiveness—both of these categories of customers are strategically aligned. Resources expended here are resources well spent as a consequence. In contrast, both Status and Streamline customers do not fall into the long-term-strategic-goals bin. These customers don't align well strategically, and so resources expended in their service are less likely to generate the kinds of long-term returns if spent on either Strategic or Star accounts. Here, rather than repeating a position already established, we seek only to reemphasize the critical importance of understanding where value can be derived, and making decisions, systematically, in accordance with this evaluation.

Top salespeople and top firms understand that not all tasks, or accounts, have the same potential to advance critical strategic goals. Top salespeople make decisions about where and how to spend their time using a calculus that explicitly encompasses movement toward goals as a key criterion. The most competitive firms also make decisions about where and how to expend scarce, account-focused resources using a very similar calculus—one that is explicitly tied to the maximization of customer lifetime value. These are not complex ideas, and the approach is not limited to the supremely gifted or well endowed. It is a philosophy that can be learned by anyone with a focus on excellence, and leveraged by anyone with a willingness to adopt a disciplined approach toward their resource-focused decisions.

In Conclusion

Our primary goal in writing this book was not to set a fad or a trend or generate hype. Nor do we want to be part of a cadre of authors seeking to blast their way into public consciousness, only to see just as quickly their ideas replaced with the next "fad," "trend," or "hype." We are not seeking to establish a new strategic mantra that salespeople are asked to adopt for several months—only to learn that the mantra was the same old tune played on a different instrument. What we are seeking to do, for now and for the future, is to establish in absolutely clear terms exactly what is necessary to become a great salesperson and a great sales organization. The ideas that can lead to greatness are the same across both levels. There is no rocket science underlying our approach—just solid, established, verified, substantiated, fact-based conclusions and cautions about the nature of the sales process that will not go out of style. Our goal is for every seasoned sales professional, newly minted business-school graduate, sales manager, account manager, account executive, sales VP, sales trainee, graduate student, and undergraduate sales student to be able to look at any page in this book and find something of value that he/she had either forgotten, not thought about in some time, or was seeing in a new way.

We want this book to be a tool that veteran salespeople can keep in the front seat of their car, glance at on the plane, or leave on their desk in order to keep at the forefront of their thinking the approach that can lead them to the absolute top of their game. Let us hear from you; share your successes and defeats at our website, www.salesandleadership.net, so we can begin a dialogue with you to develop an even larger community in our ongoing mission to transform selling.

CPSIA information can be obtained at www.ICGtesting.com
Printed in the USA
BVOW04s1336210814

363670BV00002B/2/P